D0152443

J REF 970.00497 STU
Student almanac of
Native American histor

PALM BEACH COUNTY
LIBRARY SYSTEM
3650 SUMMIT BLVD
WEST PALM BEACH, FLORIDA 33406

Student Almanac of Native American History

Volume 2: From the Trail of Tears to the Present, 1839–Today

Student Almanac of Native American History

Volume 2: From the Trail of Tears to the Present, 1839–Today

GREENWOOD PRESS
Westport, Connecticut • London

Library of Congress Cataloging-in-Publication Data
Media Projects, Inc.
Student almanac of Native American history.
p. cm.—(Middle school reference)
Includes bibliographical references and index.
ISBN 0-313-32599-5 (set: alk. paper)—ISBN 0-313-32600-2 (v. 1: alk. paper)—
ISBN 0-313-32601-0 (v. 2: alk. paper)
1. Indians of North America—History. [1. Indians of North America—History.] I. Series.
E77.S925 2003
970'.00497—dc21 2002035215

British Library Cataloguing in Publication Data is available.

Copyright © 2003 by Greenwood Publishing Group, Inc.

All rights reserved. No portion of this book may be reproduced, by any process or technique, without the express written consent of the publisher.

Library of Congress Catalog Card Number: 2002035215
ISBN: 0-313-32599-5 (set)
0-313-32600-2 (vol. 1)
0-313-32601-0 (vol. 2)

First published in 2003

Greenwood Press, 88 Post Road West, Westport, CT 06881
An imprint of Greenwood Publishing Group, Inc.
www.greenwood.com

Printed in the United States of America

The paper used in this book complies with the Permanent Paper Standard issued by the National Information Standards Organization (Z39.48-1984).

10 9 8 7 6 5 4 3 2 1

A Media Projects, Inc. Production
Contributing Writers: George Ochoa, Melinda Corey, Elin Woodger, Norman Murphy, Michele Camardella, Doreen Russo
Design: Amy Henderson
Production: Anthony Galante and Jim Burmester
Editor: Carter Smith
Indexer: Marilyn Flaig

CONTENTS

Volume 2: From the Trail of Tears to the Present, 1839–Today

From the Trail of Tears to the Present

1839–Today

"Indians remain Indian, and against pretty good odds."

—N. Scott Momaday, Kiowa novelist, 1990

To many people, Native American history brings to mind the struggle of America's first people to hold onto their lands and their way of life in the face of white settlers moving westward across the American wilderness. To these people, this struggle began when **Christopher Columbus** (see Vol. 1, p. 60) arrived in the Caribbean in 1492. To them, it ended with the massacre at **Wounded Knee** (see p. 54) in 1890. Some of the people in that story, like **Tecumseh** (see Vol. 1, p. 118), **Black Hawk** (see Vol. 1, p. 101), and **Pocahontas** (see Vol. 1, p. 79) are well known, and are among the first names people think of when they think about Native American history. Their stories took place before Native Americans were forced from the eastern United States. Their stories were the subject of the first volume of *Student Almanac of Native American History.*

Indian Wars in the West

This book, *Student Almanac of Native American History, Volume 2,* is the story of Native Americans since 1839, when the Cherokee walked the **Trail of Tears** (see Vol. 1, p. 121). Chapter 1 tells about the Indian Wars for the West, from the 1840s until 1890. This period gave rise to warriors like **Geronimo** (see p. 33) and **Crazy Horse** (see p. 31); battles like **Little Bighorn** (see p. 37); and tragedies like the Wounded Knee massacre.

As you will learn, the 1840s and 1850s were a time when the United States grew very quickly. First the U.S. annexed Texas, which had won its independence from **Mexico** (see p. 38) in 1836. Then, the United States won even more territory from Mexico, including California, New Mexico, Arizona, and other parts of the Southwest. After settling a dispute with Britain over what are now Oregon and Washington, and buying some additional land from Mexico, the United States reached its present-day continental boundaries by 1853. American settlers felt it was their "manifest destiny" or God-given right, to settle the land that, as they saw it, had been a wilderness populated by savages.

Native Americans, of course, did not think of themselves as savages, but as people with a way of life worth preserving. When white settlers began to flood into the West, the result was war.

The Indian Wars for the West broke out in many places at many times. In the 1850s, one war after another took place from Oregon and Washington to the Southwest and Great Plains. Warfare continued during the 1860s, and Native Americans continued to rise up against white settlers. This was especially true during the U.S. **Civil War** (see p. 27), when most of the United States' military was fighting in the East. To try to end the wars, the U.S. often signed temporary peace treaties with Native Americans. Usually the treaties were quickly broken by more white settlers eager for land.

By the 1870s, the United States decided it would no longer make treaties with Native American nations. Although Crazy Horse and **Sitting Bull** (see p. 47) became household names after the Sioux victory over George Armstrong Custer's troops at Little Bighorn, the Native Americans of the West were fighting a losing battle against U.S. forces. Within a year of Little Bighorn, both the Sioux and Cheyenne had surrendered.

Allotment and Assimilation

After 1890, Native Americans were largely confined to reservations. But even this land was in danger of being lost. In 1887, Congress passed the General Allotment (see **allotment policy**, p. 19) Act, which said that reservation lands, which had been owned in common by the tribes, were to be broken up into individual plots, or allotments. Each individual head of a Native American family would receive 160 acres, with surplus lands to be sold to non-Indians. The idea was to encourage Native Americans to farm their land and assimilate, or blend, into non-Indian society. The old ways of life, the government hoped, would disappear.

Chapter 2 covers Native American life in the first half of the 20th century. During this time, the allotment system left Native Americans with less land than they had had at the end of the Indian Wars. Some sold their land since they did not know how to farm, others were cheated by laws that discriminated against Native Americans. From 1887 to 1934, Native Americans lost nearly two-thirds of their land.

Allotment was only one way used to make Native Americans blend into society. Another was the banning of Native American religion. Still another was the practice of sending Native American children to **boarding schools** (see p. 68) managed or funded by the U.S. government. In these schools, children lived far away from their tribes and were not allowed to speak their native languages or practice their ancient customs.

Despite efforts to assimilate Native Americans, the policy was a failure. By the 1930s, Native Americans were the poorest group in the country, and their population at an all-time low. Many young Native Americans felt as if they had no culture, neither Native American nor European-American.

In the 1930s, the government took a new approach. The **Indian Reorganization Act** of 1934 (see p. 76) banned allotment. Most important, the U.S. recognized that tribal governments had a right to exist and encouraged Native Americans to adopt tribal constitutions and by-laws. Religious freedom was guaranteed. Reservation schools were favored over boarding schools. Economic programs were put in place to help Native Americans to prosper.

The Late 20th Century

In Chapter 3, readers will learn about how the relationship between the government and Native Americans changed again. In the past, the government had treated Native Americans as a population that it had promised to protect and support. But in 1953, Congress passed the **Termination** (see p. 119) Resolution. It said that Native Americans should be treated the same as other Americans.

During the 1960s, some Native Americans began to call for their rights. In 1968, the **American Indian Movement (AIM)** (see p. 99) was founded. AIM took part in several, sometimes violent demonstrations, including the occupation of Alcatraz Island, California, a march called the **Trail of Broken Treaties** (see p. 122), and the **siege of Wounded Knee** (see p. 124), South Dakota.

By the mid-1970s, the government recommitted itself to honoring its obligations with Native Americans. Termination policy was ended, replaced with an emphasis on **self-determination** (see p. 118), or freedom of a people to plan their own course. Native Americans emerged with a new pride in their heritage, along with greater self-confidence and readiness for political involvement.

Today, Native Americans enjoy better **health** (see p. 110), prosperity, and **education** (see p. 107) than in the past. The Native American population has grown. Traditional culture is taught to young Native Americans, and writers and artists bring it to a wider audience.

Despite their advances in the last few decades, Native Americans still face problems such as poverty, disease, and lack of educational opportunities. But Native Americans have reason to be hopeful. After centuries of hardship, Native Americans' rights have been recognized and their population is growing.

How to Use this Book

Each chapter in *Student Almanac of Native American History* is divided into two parts. The first is a short essay that gives a summary of the major events in that time in Native American history. The second is an A–Z section that describes many important people, events, and terms that have to do with the time period.

To help readers find related ideas more easily, many terms are cross-indexed. Within both the essay and A–Z section of each chapter, some words appear in **bold letters**. That means that the term is also a separate A–Z entry in *Student Almanac of Native American History*, which should be read for more information. Other unfamiliar words are printed in ***bold italics***. Short definitions of these words can be found in a glossary on page 127. Finally, words that may be hard to pronounce are followed by a pronunciation key.

CHAPTER ONE

Fight No More Forever

The Indian Wars for the West, 1839–1890

"Hear me, my chiefs. I am tired; my heart is sick and sad. From where the sun now stands I will fight no more forever."

—Chief Joseph, Nez Percé leader, after surrendering to U.S. forces, 1877

In March 1839, the **Cherokee** (see Vol. 1, p. 25) finished the long trek from Georgia that became known as the **Trail of Tears** (see Vol. 1, p. 121). They were the last of the Native American nations living east of the Mississippi River. They were removed to a new land west of the Mississippi called **Indian Territory** (see Vol. 1, p. 106), today's Oklahoma. The removal of the Native American nations to Indian Territory was supposed to bring peace between settlers and Native Americans. Instead, the wars between them in the eastern part of the country shifted to the West.

Near Indian Territory, settlers were already fighting Native Americans in the independent republic of Texas. In 1839, Texans forced many Native Americans to leave east Texas for Indian Territory. These nations included the Cherokee of Texas who were defeated at the Battle of the Neche. Other Native Americans such as the Comanche, Kiowa, and Apache stayed in Texas. They fought a war that lasted until the 1870s. These Native American nations were allied with the Cheyenne, Arapaho, and Sioux. This mighty alliance opposed U.S. expansion in the Great Plains. The conflicts in which they were involved were just some of the Indian Wars fought for control of the West.

Sometimes Native Americans and settlers lived peacefully side by side, trading with each other. Until 1871, treaties were signed in which Native Americans agreed to sell some of their land and settle on **reservations** (see p.

45). One major treaty signing took place at Fort Laramie in Wyoming in 1851. In that treaty, about 10,000 representatives of **Sioux** (see Vol. 1, p. 46), **Cheyenne** (see Vol. 1, p. 26), **Crow** (see Vol. 1, p. 30), **Arapaho** (see Vol. 1, p. 23) and other nations agreed to live in peace with American citizens. In return, the United States promised to give goods to the Native Americans once a year.

Yet treaties were always being broken and the promised goods were not distributed. Farmers, miners, and ranchers trespassed on land set aside for Native Americans. Many of the reservations were barren places that were run by corrupt agents. These conditions prompted Native Americans to leave the reservations. In the midst of many of these tensions, small-scale violence broke out, including raids, assaults, or massacres by one side or the other. The victims reacted with more violence. Full-scale war was the next step.

In the 1870s, President Ulysses S. Grant tried to stop the violence and wars. He put the reservations under the control of Christian churches. This effort was known as the **Peace Policy** (see p. 42). The policy failed and the poorly run reservations continued. In addition, the church leaders tried to do away with the religions of the Native Americans. Peace was hard to keep.

Any event could spark a war. In the Oregon country in 1847, Cayuse children at a mission school came down with measles. The disease became ***epidemic*** and the Cayuse blamed the missionaries. The Cayuse murdered the missionaries Marcus and Narcissa Whitman, along with several others. The result was the **Cayuse War** (see p. 25). It ended with the opening

Timeline

1836–1875

The **Comanche and Kiowa Wars** take place in Texas. Texas is an independent republic from 1836 until 1845, when it enters the United States.

1836–1890

Indian Wars rage throughout the West between Native Americans and people from the United States.

of Cayuse lands to settlement. That in turn led to more wars in the Northwest.

No one can say exactly how many western wars there were. Small skirmishes became larger, and those became full-scale battles. If a conflict involved several battles and reached some kind of conclusion, it might be called a war. It could also be part of a larger series of wars. For example, the Battle of the Rosebud was one part of the Sioux War for the Black Hills, which was one war among many in the Sioux Wars that lasted from 1854 to 1890.

Native Americans did not fight as a single group. Instead, each nation usually fought over a local issue, sometimes in alliance with one or more of the nations in the area. **Red Cloud's War** (see p. 44) was fought over the Bozeman Trail that cut through Oglala Sioux hunting grounds in Wyoming and Montana.

Officers such as Nelson Miles, **George Crook** (see p. 32), and Philip Henry Sheridan led U.S. Army troops involved in the wars. Sheridan is reported to have said, "The only good Indians I ever saw were dead." Sometimes only state or territorial ***militia***, or even just armed citizens, fought against the Native Americans. During the Civil War, few U.S. troops could be spared for the Indian Wars. After the Civil War ended, the troops were sent into the West in great numbers.

Native Americans won a number of battles, and at least one war, Red Cloud's War. But in the long run, U.S. forces, sometimes with the aid of

1840	1846–1848	1847	1850–1851
The Comanche, Kiowa, Apache, Cheyenne, Arapaho, and Sioux form an alliance that opposes U.S. expansion in the Great Plains.	The **Mexican-American War** brings the Native Americans of the Southwest and California under U.S. jurisdiction.	The Tiwa of Taos Pueblo revolt against U.S. rule, killing the governor of New Mexico before U.S. forces suppress the rebellion.	In the Mariposa Indian War, the Miwok and Yokut rebel over injustices stemming from the **California Gold Rush**, which began in 1849.

Native American scouts, defeated every Native American nation that they fought. The Indian Wars for the West took place in several regions: the Northwest, California, the Southwest and Great Basin, and the Great Plains.

THE NORTHWEST

The arrival of European-American settlers along the Oregon Trail, particularly in the 1840s and 1850s, sparked conflict in the Oregon country. Yet the non-Native American population of the Northwest kept growing. By 1853, the region had become so widely populated that two territories, Oregon and Washington, had been carved out of it. The governor of Washington Territory reached a peace agreement with the local Native American nations at the **Walla Walla Council** (see p. 51). Promises were made in return for the Native Americans' agreement to move onto reservations. The promises were quickly broken, and two wars broke out, the Yakima War and the Coeur d'Alene War.

Other Indian wars took place during the 1860s and 1870s. The Snake War involved the **Paiute** (*PIE-oot*) (see Vol. 1, p. 42) of Oregon and Idaho. In the **Bannock War** (see p. 21), the Paiute fought again, this time in alliance with the Bannock. In the **Nez Percé War** (see p. 41), **Chief Joseph** (see p. 36), the **Nez Percé** (see Vol. 1, p. 41) leader, tried to avoid being put on a reservation. He took his followers on a 1,000-mile journey to Canada. U.S. Army forces stopped them just south of the Canadian border and forced them to surrender.

1851

About 10,000 representatives of Great Plains nations meet at Fort Laramie in Wyoming Territory to sign the Treaty of Fort Laramie. The treaty defines territories and provides for government payments. Peace falls apart with the start of the Sioux Wars three years later.

1853

In the **Gadsden Purchase**, the United States buys from Mexico a strip of land along their mutual border. Native Americans in that region come under U.S. jurisdiction.

1853

In the Walker War, Native Americans in Utah fight Mormon settlers.

1854–1890

The Sioux Wars rage in the Northern Plains between the Sioux and U.S. forces. Early episodes include the **Santee Uprising** in Minnesota (1862).

A new frontier opened in **Alaska** (see p. 19). The United States purchased Alaska from Russia in 1867. In this new region, U.S. forces came into conflict with the **Tlingit** (see Vol. 1, p. 47) people.

California

The **Mexican-American War** (see p. 38) made California part of the United States. Gold was discovered in California in 1848. Many whites came to California to find gold and to get rich quickly. California's Native Americans were pushed aside by miners who settled on their lands. The miners were cruel to the Native Americans and brought diseases to the Native peoples. The **Miwok** (see Vol. 1, p. 38) and Yokut nations rebelled in the Mariposa Indian War. Another rebellion occurred when the **Modoc** (see Vol. 1, p. 39) in northern California revolted against being moved onto a reservation.

The Southwest and Great Basin

The end of the Mexican-American War brought the United States possession of the Southwest and Great Basin. Along with the land, the U.S. took over the bad relations that Mexico had had with Native Americans there. The Tewa of Taos **Pueblo** (see Vol. 1, p. 44) killed the U.S. governor of New Mexico. U.S. troops struck back and killed many Native Americans. The **Navajo** (see Vol. 1, p. 41) of New Mexico resisted U.S. rule. The conflicts

1855	1857–1879	1860	1861–1865
At the **Walla Walla Council**, Native Americans in Washington Territory reach a peace agreement with the territorial governor. The collapse of the agreement leads to more wars.	The **Cheyenne Wars** pit the Cheyenne of the Great Plains against the United States.	In the Pyramid Lake War, the Northern Paiute of western Nevada fight U.S. forces.	Native Americans fight on both sides of the **Civil War**.

increased in the **Navajo War** (see p. 40). In this war, **Kit Carson** (see p. 25) forced the Navajo to surrender. Many died on a 300-mile "Long Walk" to the site of their reservation.

In the **Apache Wars** (see p. 21), the **Apache** (see Vol. 1, p. 22) of Arizona and New Mexico fought U.S. forces. Apache leaders such as **Cochise** (see p. 28) and **Geronimo** (see p. 33) were among the strongest enemies against U.S. rule. After escaping from captivity more than once, Geronimo finally surrendered. His surrender ended the Apache Wars.

Nevada and Utah, part of the Great Basin region, also saw action in the Indian Wars. In Utah, Native Americans had good relations with the Mormons. The Mormons were European-American members of a new religion who migrated to Utah. However, there were clashes, such as the Walker War. In it, the Mormons fought a band of **Ute** (see Vol. 1, p. 47). The Northern Paiute of western Nevada took up arms in the **Pyramid Lake War** (see p. 44).

The Great Plains

It was on the Great Plains after the Civil War that the Indian Wars entered their final phase. U.S. Army troops had experience in Civil War battles. They now fought against the horse-riding warriors of the Great Plains nations. These nations were known by their Native American enemies as "the best fighters the sun ever shone on." The U.S. Army was equipped with artillery that was advanced for its day and could kill many enemies at once.

1861–1866	1862	1863–1866	1866–1868
In the **Apache Wars**, the Apache resist U.S. forces in the Southwest.	The Homestead Act offers a 160-acre plot of land in the West to anyone who will inhabit it for five years. The act speeds white settlement of the West.	In the **Navajo War**, the Navajo rebel against U.S. rule in Arizona and New Mexico. Defeated, the Navajo are forced to go on a 300-mile "Long Walk" (1864).	In **Red Cloud's War**, Sioux and Northern Cheyenne forces led by Red Cloud force the U.S. Army to give up forts in Wyoming and Montana.

In the southern Plains, the **Comanche** (see Vol. 1, p. 29) and **Kiowa** (see Vol. 1, p. 36) nations continued their war with the people of Texas. The Comanche were led by warriors such as **Quanah Parker** (see p. 42), and the Kiowa by men such as Satanta and Satank. The end of the **Comanche and Kiowa Wars** (see p. 29) came in the **Red River War** (see p. 44). This war was fought in Texas, Kansas, Colorado, and New Mexico. In Colorado, the Cheyenne and **Arapaho** (see Vol. 1, p. 23) fought frequently with the United States, notably in the **Colorado War** (see p. 28).

The **Sioux** (see Vol. 1, p. 46) of the Northern Plains were the last Native American people to clash with the U.S. military. The Sioux Wars began in Wyoming in 1854, and continued until 1890. In Minnesota, the Santee Sioux led the **Santee Uprising** (see p. 46). A gold rush to the Black Hills of South Dakota sparked the Sioux War for the Black Hills. During that conflict, the **Battle of Little Bighorn** (see p. 37) was fought. The Sioux and Cheyenne, led by **Crazy Horse** (see p. 31) and **Sitting Bull** (see p. 47), defeated the entire command of Lieutenant Colonel **George Armstrong Custer** (see p. 32). More troops were sent to replace the ones lost, and the Sioux and Cheyenne surrendered shortly afterward.

The Indian Wars ended with a bloody massacre by U.S. forces at a Sioux camp at **Wounded Knee** (see p. 54), South Dakota. It was fought because of tensions over the new Sioux **Ghost Dance religion** (see p. 34). The religion, which combined dancing, singing, praying, chanting, and

1871	1874–1875	1876–1877	1877
Congress declares that treaties will no longer be made with Native Americans.	In the Red River War, an alliance of Comanche, Kiowa, Cheyenne, and Arapaho battle U.S. forces in the Great Plains.	The Sioux War for the Black Hills takes place. Led by **Crazy Horse** and **Sitting Bull**, the Sioux wipe out the command of Lieutenant Colonel George Armstrong Custer in the **Battle of Little Bighorn**. But the Sioux lose the war.	In the **Nez Percé War**, **Chief Joseph** resists efforts to place the Nez Percé on a reservation by trying to lead them to Canada.

meditating, was based on the the idea that one day, non-Native Americans would disappear from the world.

In the 1890s, there were occasional raids or outbreaks of violence, but for the most part the Indian Wars were over. Defeated in war, Native Americans settled down to an unhappy peace on their **reservations** (see p. 45). The reservations were getting smaller as the federal government divided the reservations into individual plots, or allotments. This was done in an effort to weaken tribal ties. Many European Americans thought that Native Americans would no longer exist as a distinct people. In this, they were wrong.

1878	1882–1886	1887	1890
In the **Bannock War**, an alliance of Native Americans, including the Bannock, Northern Paiute, and Cayuse, fight U.S. forces in Oregon and Idaho.	U.S. forces fight the Apache in the Southwest, in the final stages of the Apache Wars. Apache leader **Geronimo** surrenders in 1886.	The General Allotment Act (see **allotment policy**), or Dawes Severalty Act, permits Native American land to be split into allotments, or shares of land to be distributed to heads of Native American families.	The **Ghost Dance religion** spreads across reservations. Fearful of rebellion related to the Ghost Dance, U.S. forces massacre about 200 Sioux at **Wounded Knee**, South Dakota. The incident is the last military clash in the Indian Wars for the West.

A-Z of Key People, Events, and Terms

Alaska

State of the United States. Alaska is located in the northwest part of North America. Russia claimed the territory that became Alaska in the 18th century. In 1867, the United States purchased it from Russia for $7.2 million. It was under military rule until 1884. During that time, there were violent periods between the **Tlingit** (*TLING-git*) (see Vol. 1, p. 47), a Native American people, and U.S. forces.

In the Kake War, a band of Tlingit people known as the Kake attacked traders. U.S. forces responded by destroying several Tlingit villages. The United States briefly withdrew its forces from Alaska. Later, fighting broke out in Sitka between Native Americans and Europeans. This fighting led the U.S. Navy to retake control of the area.

The Tlingit again went to war, this time over the killing of a Tlingit shaman, or holy person. The U.S. Navy bombed the Tlingit village of Angoon (*an-GOON*) and ended the uprising. In 1973, long after 1959 when Alaska had become a state, the federal government paid $90,000 to settle a Tlingit lawsuit over the bombing.

allotment policy

Federal government plan to break up Native American lands into individual plots, or allotments. Each Native American nation had owned its reservation land. In 1887, Congress passed the General Allotment Act, or Dawes Severalty Act. The act was named for its sponsor, Senator Henry Dawes. It gave lands belonging to Native American nations to individual Native Americans. Each Native American head of a family received 160 acres of land. All lands unclaimed by Native Americans were to be sold to non-Native Americans. The hope was that the Native American landowners would farm their land and blend into the general society. In this way, Native Americans would lose their ties to old Native American ways of life.

Why Allotment?

Carl Schurz was the Secretary of the Interior. Soon after leaving that post, he wrote an article saying that Native Americans faced a "stern alternative: extermination or civilization." To help civilize them, he argued, lands owned in common by Indian tribes should be broken up and distributed to individual Indians, for them to farm as their own personal property. This policy, called allotment, became law six years later, with the General Allotment Act (1887). Schurz's article is excerpted below.

When the Indians have become individual property owners, holding their farms by the same title under the law by which white men hold theirs, they will feel more readily inclined to part with such of their lands as they can not themselves cultivate, and from which they can derive profit only if they sell them, either in lots or in bulk, for a fair equivalent in money or in annuities. This done, the Indians will occupy no more ground than so many white people; the large reservations will gradually be opened to general settlement and enterprise, and the Indians, with their possessions, will cease to stand in the way of the "development of the country." The difficulty which has provoked so many encroachments and conflicts will then no longer exist. When the Indians are individual owners of real property, and as individuals enjoy the protection of the laws, their tribal cohesion will necessarily relax, and gradually disappear. They will have advanced an immense step in the direction of the "white man's way."

Source: Carl Schurz, "Present Aspects of the Indian Problem," *North American Review*.

Along with allotment policy, other actions tried to make Native Americans give up their old ways of life. One of these actions was the use of boarding schools that were run by the federal government. The Carlisle Indian School, founded in Pennsylvania in 1879, became a model for boarding schools. At Carlisle, Native American children lived far away from home. They were not allowed to speak their native languages or to practice their native customs.

Allotment policy turned out to be very harmful to Native Americans. Native American nations lost much of their territory. The unclaimed individual plots were sold to non-Native Americans. Sometimes the land Native Americans were allotted was not good for farming. Most Native Americans did not know how to farm it. Native American owners often sold their plots to land speculators. These were people who made a living from buying and selling land. The speculators coaxed, cheated, and bullied Native Americans into giving up much of their territory. During the period when allotment policy was in force, Native Americans lost nearly two-thirds of the total land they had held in 1887.

Allotment policy came to an end in 1934 with the Indian Reorganization Act, or Wheeler-Howard Act. It banned further allotment of Native American lands.

Apache Wars

Military conflicts between the **Apache** (see Vol. 1, p. 22) and Americans in the Southwest occurring between 1861 and 1886. Throughout their history, the Apache had raided Pueblo, Spanish, Mexican, and American settlements. In 1861, **Cochise** (see p. 28), chief of the Chiricahua (*cheer-ee-CAH-wuh*) band of Apache, was arrested. Cochise escaped, but other Apache were taken hostage. Cochise fought back by taking American hostages. This began 25 years of warfare between the Apache and Americans.

The Apache struck with quick raids and ambushes. Then they would retreat to their mountain hideouts. U.S. forces built forts and fought the Apache through open battle, trickery, and massacre.

Gradually, the Apache agreed to move onto reservations. This happened when U.S. forces won decisive battles in the Tonto Basin Campaign in Arizona. Reservation life became too harsh for the Apache. Many went back to fighting on both the Mexican and U.S. sides of the border.

Two war leaders became especially famous: Victorio, an Apache chief, led an uprising from 1877 to 1880; and **Geronimo** (see p. 33), a Chiricahua Apache chief, led another rebellion from 1881 to 1886. Victorio died in the Battle of Tres Castillos (*trace cah-STEE-yos*) in Mexico. Geronimo was captured twice, but escaped both times. In 1886, Geronimo finally surrendered to General Nelson Miles. He never again took up fighting. There were a few raids by other Apache bands into the 1890s, but for the most part the Apache Wars were over.

Bannock War

Military conflict in Oregon and Idaho between U.S. forces and Native Americans in 1878. Native American nations involved in the conflicts were the **Bannock** (see Vol. 1, p. 24), Northern **Paiute** (*PIE-oot*) (see Vol. 1, p. 42), Cayuse (*KYE-oose*), and **Umatilla** (*oom-uh-TILL-uh*) (see Vol. 1, p. 47). In 1863, the Bannock and **Shoshone** (*sho-SHO-nee*) (see Vol. 1, p.45) of the Great Basin were defeated in the Bear River Campaign. This was also known as the Shoshone War. It was fought in Utah and Idaho. The Bannock were sent to a reservation in Idaho. Many white settlers also came onto the reservation land, but the food the government promised the Bannock did not.

A group of Bannock and Paiute rebelled and left the reservation. Other Native Americans joined them. U.S. general Oliver O. Howard defeated them in battle and ended the uprising.

Black Kettle

Southern **Cheyenne** (see Vol. 1, p. 26) chief who wanted peace with settlers. Black Kettle (1803-1868) led his people to settle at Sand Creek, Colorado. He told Colonel John Chivington at the nearby army post that he wanted peace, but Chivington attacked Black Kettle's camp. More than 200 Native Americans died in what was called the Sand Creek Massacre. Black Kettle continued to speak out for peace to both his own warriors and U.S. officers. He settled on the Washita River near what is now Cheyenne, Oklahoma. There he suffered another surprise attack. Lieutenant Colonel George Armstrong Custer led this attack. Black Kettle and many of his people died. This attack was part of General Philip Sheridan's successful plan against the Cheyenne. It was known as the Southern Plains War.

Billy Bowlegs
(Library of Congress)

Bowlegs, Billy

Seminole (see Vol. 1, p. 116) leader. Bowlegs led his people in Florida in an uprising in the Third **Seminole War** (see Vol. 1, p. 117). At the end of the war, he and his band agreed to migrate west. In the **Civil War** (see p. 27), Billy Bowlegs led Seminole warriors in fighting on the Union side.

buffalo, destruction of

Native Americans of the Great Plains **culture area** (see Vol. 1, p. 30) depended on the American buffalo. They hunted buffalo for food and clothing and to make tools from their bones, skin, and

Unlike Native Americans, who relied on the buffalo for food, clothing, and more, whites often hunted buffalo for sport. Wealthy hunters often killed buffalo from moving trains, leaving their dead bodies to rot, rather than use any of their meat or skin for other purposes. (Library of Congress)

muscles. In the mid-1800s, it is estimated that 75 million buffalo roamed across the Great Plains. Beginning in the 1860s, non-Native Americans killed them in large numbers. They used the buffalo for food, especially to feed railroad crews. They also killed the buffalo for their hides. As the cattle industry developed after the **Civil War** (see p. 27), cattle diseases spread to the buffalo. These diseases killed the buffalo in great numbers. The government wanted to destroy the buffalo herds. It thought that destroying the herds would leave its Native American enemies without a main source of food. The U.S. could then force the Native Americans to move to reservations. By 1889, only 541 buffalo could be counted in the United States. Legislative and private efforts then began to try to keep the buffalo from becoming extinct. Thanks to these measures, tens of thousands of buffalo still survive.

California Gold Rush

The mass *migration* of people to California after the discovery of gold. The Maidu (*MAY-du*) Native Americans worked for James

After gold was discovered at Sutter's Mill in California, thousands of miners poured into California. (Library of Congress)

Marshall, the man credited with the first California gold discovery. The Maidu discovered gold in 1848 at Sutter's Mill near Sacramento, California. Native Americans made up at least half of those working the mines. Non-Native American miners began to come to California in 1849 and take over the mining jobs. The new miners thought of the Native Americans as competitors. Later, settlers came and wanted the Native American lands. The number of non-native Californians grew quickly from 15,000 in 1848 to about 93,000 in 1850. This was the year that California became a state.

Many miners came to California from the eastern U.S. over the California Trail. Others followed the Southern Overland Trail. At first, the Yuma Nation kept them from entering California. The Yuma controlled the Yuma Crossing. This crossing allowed passage across the Colorado River. The U.S. tried to build forts to keep the crossing open. The Yuma, the Mojave (*mo-HAHV-ee*), and several other native peoples joined in a revolt against the settlers. The revolt was called the Yuma and Mojave Uprising.

Another uprising of the time was the Mariposa Indian War. It was fought with the Miwok (*MEE-wok*) and Yokuts (*yo-CUTS*) against the miners. The miners had been mining on Native American lands and treating the people violently.

Despite this resistance, Native Americans were not able to stop the non–Native Americans. Many of the miners who came in the Gold Rush remained in California. They settled on Native American lands. This period extended to the time of the Colorado Gold Rush. It marked one of the heaviest periods of European settlement on Native American land in U.S. history. It also reduced the number of Native Americans in the area. By the end of the 1850s, their number was reduced from about 50,000 to about 30,000.

Carson, Christopher "Kit"

American explorer, trapper, and scout. Carson (1809–1868) was born in Madison County, Kentucky. He joined the Santa Fe expedition to modern-day New Mexico. Later, he traveled with John Frémont through California as a trapper and a guide. Carson served as the U.S. Indian agent to the **Ute** (see Vol. 1 p. 47). He became famous in the **Mexican-American War** (see p. 38) at the battle of San Pascual (*pas-KAL*).

Kit Carson
(Library of Congress)

In the **Civil War** (see p. 27), Carson led the 1st New Mexico Volunteers in fighting the region's Native Americans. He placed hundreds of Mescalero **Apache** (see Vol. 1, p. 22) on New Mexico's Bosque (*bosk*) Redondo Reserve and captured over 12,000 **Navajo** (see Vol. 1, p. 41). The capture followed a six-month action that included destroying Navajo food sources and their way of life.

Carson headed the Bosque Redondo Reservation near Fort Sumner. At this reservation, the Native Americans were to be retrained as farmers. After the war, he worked as an ***Indian agent***. His autobiography is *Kit Carson's Own Story of His Life* (1926).

Cayuse (*KYE-use*) War

Military conflict (1847-1850) between the Cayuse and non-Native Americans in the Oregon country. In 1847, missionaries worked among the Cayuse. A measles ***epidemic*** broke out that killed hundreds of Cayuse. The Cayuse blamed the missionaries for bringing the disease. They attacked the mission of Marcus and Narcissa Whitman. The mission was located near present-day Walla Walla, Washington. The Cayuse killed the Whitmans and others and took hostages. The result of this attack was the first of many Native American Wars in the Pacific Northwest.

A volunteer army of non-Indian settlers retaliated for the massacre at the mission. The army attacked a Cayuse camp and killed about 30 people. Congress then created the Oregon Territory and added more military posts. The war ended in 1850, when five Cayuse were convicted and hanged for the Whitman murders.

Cheyenne Wars

Military conflicts between the **Cheyenne** (see Vol. 1, p. 26) and the United States that took place from 1857 to 1879. The Cheyenne were Native Americans of the Great Plains. They were divided into the Southern Cheyenne and the Northern Cheyenne. Both groups tried to stop U.S. expansion into their lands. The Southern Cheyenne were allied to the Arapaho and other Plains Nations. The first major clash between the Southern Cheyenne and the U.S. was the Battle of Solomon Fork in Kansas. The battle was won by U.S. troops under Colonel Edwin Sumner. The next clash was the Colorado War. It began with a massacre of peaceful Cheyenne at Sand Creek, Colorado (see **Black Kettle**, p. 22).

Next was General Winfield Scott Hancock's actions against the Southern Cheyenne and their **Sioux** (see Vol. 1, p. 46) allies in Kansas, Colorado, and Nebraska. The Southern Plains War followed this. In this war, General Philip Henry Sheridan made a surprise U.S. attack on the Washita River in Oklahoma.

U.S. troops and Cheyenne warriors fought a long series of battles between 1857 and 1879. (Library of Congress)

The Northern Cheyenne fought as Sioux allies in the Sioux Wars. These included **Red Cloud's War** (see p. 44) and the **Battle of Little Bighorn** (see p. 37). The Northern Cheyenne surrendered in 1877. They were sent to a **reservation** (see p. 45) in Indian Territory. There, hunger and disease plagued them. A *band* led by Dull Knife and Little Wolf escaped and tried to return to their homelands in Wyoming and Montana. Known as the Flight of the Northern Cheyenne, this attempted journey failed. The surviving Northern Cheyenne eventually received a reservation in their homeland.

Chisholm, Jesse

American frontier leader. Chisholm (1806?-1868) was born in Tennessee to a Scottish-American trader and **Cherokee** (see Vol. 1, p. 25) mother. He moved as a child to the Arkansas River area near Fort Smith, Oklahoma. After the 1821 opening of the Santa Fe Trail, he served as a guide and interpreter for the U.S. military. Chisholm also helped to lead expeditions and set up trading posts in Comanche and Kiowa (*KYE-uh-wuh*) territory. This territory was in modern-day Oklahoma and northern Texas.

During the Civil War, Chisholm joined forces with Native American nations in southern Oklahoma who had remained neutral during the war. After the war, he was active in setting up trade between Abilene, Kansas, and Mexico. Settlers traded goods with the Kiowa and Comanche for buffalo hides along Chisholm's wagon trail. In 1867, this trail was used for cattle drives and became known as the Chisholm Trail.

Civil War

Military conflict between the Northern U.S. (the Union) and the Southern U.S. (the Confederacy). The Civil War began in 1861 when the eleven states of the Confederacy broke away from the United States and tried to establish their own government. The main issue was slavery. The southern economy depended on slavery. Many northerners considered slavery immoral.

East of the Mississippi, Native Americans fought on both sides of the conflict. These nations included members of the **Caddo** (see Vol. 1, p. 24), **Creek** (see Vol. 1, p. 29), **Delaware** (see Vol. 1, p. 30), Seneca, and **Shawnee** (see Vol. 1, p. 45). The Confederacy was more successful than the Union at recruiting Native Americans. They recruited mostly from **Indian Territory** (see Vol. 1, p. 106). In Indian Territory, some Native Americans owned African slaves. The **Cherokee** (see Vol. 1, p. 25) formed an alliance with the Confederacy. The Creek were split. Some Creek warriors fought against the Confederates, while others fought for them.

Some Civil War fighting took place west of the Mississippi. Union forces recaptured Indian Territory. In Texas, the Confederacy urged the **Comanche** (see Vol. 1, p. 29) and **Kiowa** (see Vol. 1, p. 36) to attack the Union. In 1864, the Comanche and Kiowa clashed with Union colonel **Christopher "Kit" Carson** (see p. 25) at Adobe Walls. But for most Native Americans in the West, the war was a distant rumor. For them, the main importance of the Civil War was that it slowed the westward flow of settlers. It also meant that U.S. Army troops moved to the East. This movement of troops weakened the federal troops fighting Native Americans in the West. It was easier for several Native American nations to raid or rise up against settlers. These nations included the **Apache** (see Vol. 1, p. 22) and **Navajo** (see Vol. 1, p. 41) in the Southwest; the Santee **Sioux** (see Vol. 1, p. 46) in the **Santee Uprising** (see p. 46) in Minnesota; and the Cheyenne in the **Colorado War** (see below). Native American warriors still faced resistance during the Civil War. This resistance came from state and territorial ***militia***. After the war, the westward movement of settlers and federal forces began again.

Cochise *(coh-CHEES)*

Chiricahua *(cheer-ee-CAH-wuh)* **Apache** (see Vol. 1, p. 22) chief. Cochise (1812-1874) was born in Arizona or New Mexico. He maintained peaceful relations with settlers through the mid-19th century. After the U.S. Army accused him of kidnapping, he took many violent actions against the army and settlers. Among these actions were raids and the taking and killing of hostages. He was not captured for nearly 10 years. He later surrendered to the U.S. Army. Cochise escaped and remained free until he bargained for a **reservation** (see p. 45) on ancestral lands.

Colorado War

Military conflict between the United States and Native Americans in Colorado. In the 1860s, a large number of miners came to

Colorado seeking gold and silver. The miners fought skirmishes with local Native Americans over use of their hunting grounds. The warfare increased with the territorial militia under Colonel John Chivington. He fought the Cheyenne, Arapaho, Sioux, **Comanche** (see Vol. 1, p. 29), and **Kiowa** (see Vol. 1, p. 36) in Colorado and Kansas. An uneasy agreement was reached. Cheyenne chief **Black Kettle** (see p. 22) settled at Sand Creek, Colorado, near Fort Lyon. He believed settling near an army post would help to keep his people safe. Chivington led a surprise attack on Black Kettle. This attack was known as the Sand Creek Massacre.

After the massacre, the Native Americans fought back again. They raided settlements and stagecoach stations. Army forces were sent to the region to stop the Native American raids. Chivington was found guilty by Congress and forced to resign for his role in the Sand Creek Massacre.

Comanche and Kiowa Wars

Military conflicts lasting from 1836 to 1875 between people from the United States and the **Comanche** (see Vol. 1, p. 29) and **Kiowa** (see Vol. 1, p. 36) Nations. Texas won its independence from Mexico in 1836. The relations between the Comanche and Kiowa and Mexico were filled with conflict. These bad relations now belonged to the new republic of Texas. The Native Americans were losing their hunting grounds to settlers. They began raiding the settlements of the non-Native Americans. The Texas Rangers were formed as a volunteer militia to fight the Comanche. The war increased with the Council House Fight. This

Cochise Speaks

After the Civil War, Chiricahua Apache leader Cochise spoke at a peace council held at the Indian agency at Canada Alamosa, New Mexico. There, to U.S. General Gordon Granger and others, he asked to remain in Arizona rather than be removed to a reservation. Later, when this request was refused, Cochise again took up arms.

When God made the world he gave one part to the white man and another to the Apache. Why was it? Why did they come together? When I was young I walked all over the country, east and west, and saw no other people than the Apaches. After many summers I walked again and found another race of people had come to take it. How is it? Why is it that the Apaches wait to die—that they carry their lives on their finger nails? The Apaches were once a great nation; they are now but a few, and because of this they want to die and so carry their lives on their finger nails. Many have been killed in battle. I have no father or mother; I am alone in the world. No one cares for Cochise; that is why I do not care to live, and wish the rocks to fall on me and cover me up.... I do not want to leave here.

Source: Kansas State Historical Collections.

was an attack on the Comanche by the Texans. The Comanche had come to the San Antonio ***council house*** to attend what they had thought would be a peace conference. After the surprise attack by the Texans, the Comanche increased their attacks.

The Texans won some battles, such as the Battle of Plum Creek. The Comanche mostly relied on horse-mounted, hit-and-run attacks that were difficult to prevent or resist. The Kiowa also carried out many attacks along the Santa Fe Trail to New Mexico. When Texas was admitted to the United States, U.S. Army troops joined the fight.

During the **Civil War** (see p. 27), the Comanche and Kiowa aided the Confederate states. They suffered a defeat from Union colonel **Christopher "Kit" Carson** (see p. 25) at Adobe Walls. Most of the Comanche and Kiowa signed a peace treaty at Medicine Lodge Creek, Kansas. They agreed to relocate to **Indian Territory** (see Vol. 1, p. 106). Some continued to resist, including **Quanah** (*KWAH-nuh*) **Parker** (see p. 42), a Comanche chief, and the Kiowa chiefs Satank, Satanta, and Lone Wolf.

Population of Native American Nations in Texas, 1690-1890

By 1890, the population of the Comanche in Texas was a mere fraction of what it had been two centuries earlier. War, disease, and forced migration had reduced the number of Comanche. Yet their numbers fell less sharply than those of some other Native American nations in Texas. This chart shows the relative population decline of those Indian nations in Texas that are believed to have numbered 2,500 or more in 1690. (The Kiowa, allies of the Comanche in the 19th century, had not yet migrated to Texas at that time.)

Nation	Population in 1690	Population in 1890
Caddo	8,500	536
Comanche	7,000	1,598
Wichita	3,200	358

Source: U.S. Census Bureau.

Sioux leader Crazy Horse was one of the greatest Native American warriors in history. Since no photograph or drawing of him was ever taken during his life, no one knows exactly what he looked like. However, in 1939, the Sioux invited sculptor Henry Korzak to begin work on the monument in South Dakota shown above. The finished model in the foreground of the picture shows what the carving on the side of the mountain in the background will look like when it is finished. When done, the statue will be larger than Mount Rushmore. (South Dakota Department of Tourism)

The Comanche and Kiowa Wars came to an end with the Red River War. It involved Cheyenne and Arapaho, and spread from Texas to Kansas, Colorado, and New Mexico. The Comanche and Kiowa defeat in that war brought an end to their resistance.

Crazy Horse

Oglala (*ahg-LAH-lah*) **Sioux** (see Vol. 1, p. 46) chief. Crazy Horse, who was born in about 1842, was considered the greatest Sioux leader. He was born in South Dakota. Crazy Horse was a great warrior, but was also known as a thinker. He was active in the fighting against the United States to keep the Black Hills for the Sioux. He was named a "shirt wearer," meaning a defender of the people, and fought in much of **Red Cloud's War** (see p. 44). In 1876, he became the supreme war and peace chief of the Oglala. That year he led his forces to victory in the battles of Rosebud and **Little Bighorn** (see p. 37). He surrendered to U.S. forces and died in 1877.

General George Crook (Library of Congress)

Crook, George

American soldier. Crook (1828-1890) graduated from West Point and fought on the Union side in the Civil War. After the war, he became known as one of the army's greatest Indian fighters. He successfully fought the **Paiute** (see Vol. 1, p. 42) in the Pacific Northwest and the **Apache** (see Vol. 1, p. 22) in Arizona Territory. In Montana the **Sioux** (see Vol. 1, p. 46) and **Cheyenne** (see Vol. 1, p. 26), led by **Crazy Horse** (see p. 31), defeated him in the Battle of Rosebud. Crook returned to Arizona, where Apache leader **Geronimo** (see p. 33) repeatedly escaped his pursuit. Crook was replaced with General Nelson Miles, who finally captured Geronimo. In his later years, Crook spoke out for the Native Americans. He condemned settlers who claimed the Native American lands. He also disagreed with the government's attempts to get the Lakota Sioux to accept **allotment policy** (see p. 19).

Custer, George Armstrong

See Little Big Horn, Battle of

De Smet, Pierre Jean *(pee-AIR jhahn de SMAY)*

Belgian-born American missionary (1801-1873). De Smet arrived in the United States in 1821 and became a Jesuit priest. He founded missions for the **Flathead** (see Vol. 1, p. 33) including St. Mary's Mission near Missoula, Montana. He worked to make peace between the U.S. government and Native Americans. He took part in the 1851 treaty council at Fort Laramie, Wyoming. At the council, he made a temporary peace with **Sitting Bull** (see p. 47). De Smet also wrote books about Native Americans and mission life. Among his books are *Letters and Sketches, with a Narrative among the Indian Tribes of the Rocky Mountains* and *Western Missions and Missionaries*.

Edenshaw, Charles

Haida (*HI-duh*) artist. Edenshaw was born in Queen Charlotte Islands, British Columbia in 1839. He belonged to the Eagle Clan of the **Haida** (see Vol. 1, p. 33). He began carving at age 14. He practiced as a carver and became expert at working in wood and argillite. Argillite is a soft black carbon-like slate material. Also working in precious metals, he became known as an important Northwest Coast Native American carver. His work shows many aspects of Haida life. Over the years, anthropologists such as Franz Boas and Charles R. Swanton met with Edenshaw. They wanted to learn of Haida art and way of life. Artist Bill Davidson is the great-grandson of Edenshaw. Edenshaw died in 1924.

Gadsden Purchase

U.S. land purchase. In 1853, American James Gadsden bargained with Mexico for the sale of about 30,000 square miles of land. The land was located along the border between Mexico and the U.S. in Arizona and New Mexico. The cost was $10 million. This purchase settled some issues remaining from the treaty that had ended the **Mexican-American War** (see p. 38). For example, it identified the exact location of the border between the countries. It ended U.S. responsibility for Native American raids into Mexico. It also brought the United States valuable land on which to build a southern transcontinental railroad. The purchase of the land brought the Native American peoples of that region under U.S. rule. With the Gadsden Purchase, the United States expanded to the shape it now has in the 48 connecting states.

Geronimo (*juh-RON-i-mo*)

Chiricahua (*cheer-ee-CAH-wuh*) **Apache** (see Vol. 1, p. 22) war chief (c. 1829-1909). Geronimo was born in Arizona. He began to raid U.S. settlements after his family was killed in 1858. Geronimo was a famous warrior. When the Chiricahua **reservation** (see p. 45) was closed, he led a group into Mexico. He was captured and escaped two times. He spent 18 months raiding and rebelling against the U.S. Army. General Nelson Miles convinced him to surrender. Geronimo was placed on a Florida reservation and was later moved to a reservation near Fort Sill, Oklahoma. He converted to Christianity and became a farmer. By selling photographs of himself,

Geronimo, one of the most famous Native American warriors of history, is seen here, far right, with several of his fellow Apache following their capture. (National Archives)

he became a nationally known figure. He appeared at President Theodore Roosevelt's inaugural procession, the 1904 World's Fair, and at patriotic celebrations. In 1906, he published an autobiography, *Geronimo's Story of His Life.*

Wovoka, a Paiute spiritual leader, founded the Ghost Dance religion in the 1880s. (Smithsonian Institution)

Ghost Dance religion

Native American spiritual movement. In the late 1880s, a Nevada **Paiute** (see Vol. 1, p. 42) named Wovoka (*wuh-VOH-kuh*) claimed he had a visit with the Supreme Being. Wovoka promised a future in which the world would end, non-Native Americans would disappear, and the earth would be restored to Native Americans. Native Americans had to live a pure life, resist the ways of the non-Native Americans, and dance in a ritual called the Ghost Dance. Ghost Dance ceremonies included dancing, singing, praying, chanting, and meditating. The Ghost Dance religion spread quickly among the peoples of the Far West, Southwest, and Great Plains. These regions include the nations of the Arapaho, Cheyenne, and several bands of Sioux. Some groups, such as the Lakota Sioux, viewed the message Wovoka received as a call to arms. They believed that their coverings, called Ghost Dance Shirts, would stop bullets. The U.S. government was frightened by the movement's popularity. The Ghost Dance was banned on reservations. In 1890, a clash with followers of the Ghost Dance began the events that led to the **Wounded Knee Massacre** (see p. 54). Many Sioux died at the massacre. After the incident at Wounded Knee, many followers of the Ghost Dance religion quickly stopped its practice.

Jackson, Helen Hunt

American author, poet. Jackson (1830-1885) was born Helen Maria Fiske in Amherst, Massachusetts. She began writing after the death of her first husband, Edward Hunt. Jackson later married William Jackson and moved to Colorado Springs, Colorado. There, she wrote about and criticized U.S. treatment of Native Americans. Her novel *Ramona* was a best-selling book. It told the story of non-Native American and Native American intermarriage. It also told about U.S. Native American policies. Another book was the nonfiction work titled *A Century of Dishonor*. This book stirred public interest in Native American rights. It condemned U.S. injustices toward Native Americans. In 1882,

Helen Hunt Jackson
(Library of Congress)

"Shameful U.S. Policy"

In her 1881 condemnation of U.S. policy toward Native Americans, *A Century of Dishonor*, writer Helen Hunt Jackson detailed the "cruelties and outrage" that Native Americans had suffered. Later in the document, which she sent to every member of Congress, she also noted how the policy must be changed.

However great perplexity and difficulty there may be in the details of any and every plan possible for doing at this late day anything like justice to the Indian, however hard it may be for good statesmen and good men to agree upon the things that ought to be done, there certainly is, or ought to be, no perplexity whatever, in agreeing upon certain things that ought not to be done before the first steps can be taken toward righting the wrongs, curing the ills, and wiping out the disgrace to us of the present condition of our Indians.

Cheating, robbing, breaking promises — these three are clearly things which must cease to be done. One more thing, also, and that is the refusal of the protection of the law to the Indian's rights of property, "of life, liberty, and the pursuit of happiness."

Source: Helen Hunt Jackson, *A Century of Dishonor*.

Jackson was named special commissioner for investigating U.S. treatment of California's Mission Indians. Jackson also wrote under the pen names of H.H. and Saxe Holm.

Joseph, Chief

Chief Joseph
(National Archives)

Nez Percé (*nez-pur-SAY*) chief. Chief Joseph (1840–1904) led a ***band*** of Nez Percé. These Native Americans refused to move from their homeland in the Wallowa area of northeastern Oregon to a reservation in Idaho. After they were threatened with military force, Chief Joseph agreed to move. Others began to fight in what was called the **Nez Percé War** (see p. 41). During the war, Joseph led his followers on a 1,000-mile trek to Canada. They fought enemy forces for more than three months. General Nelson Miles, near the Bear Paw Mountains just south of Canada, finally defeated Chief Joseph. The Nez Percé surrendered and were forced to move to Oklahoma. Chief Joseph begged for his people to be

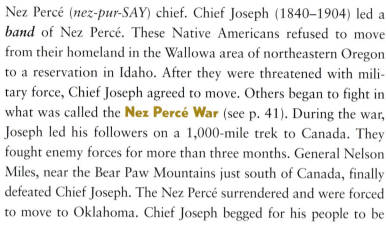

Chief Joseph Surrenders

At the end of the Nez Percé War (1877), Nez Percé leader Chief Joseph surrendered to Colonel Nelson Miles, representing General Oliver Howard. By that time, most of the chiefs of the Nez Percé had been killed in battle, including Looking Glass and Toohoolhoolzote (*too-hool-hool-ZOH-tay*). In his surrender, Joseph expressed the weariness of all Native Americans who defended their land valiantly only to lose in the end.

Tell General Howard I know his heart. What he told me before, I have in my heart.

I am tired of fighting. Our chiefs are killed. Looking Glass is dead. Toohoolhoolzote is dead. The old men are all dead.

It is the young men who say yes and no. He who led on the young men is dead. It is cold and we have no blankets. The little children are freezing to death.

My people, some of them, have run away to the hills, and have no blankets, no food; no one knows where they are —perhaps freezing to death. I want to have time to look for my children and see how many I can find. Maybe I shall find them among the dead.

Hear me, my chiefs. I am tired; my heart is sick and sad. From where the sun now stands I will fight no more forever.

Source: *Harper's Weekly*, 1877.

permitted to return to their homeland. They were allowed to return to a reservation in Washington, though not to the Wallowa area. Both Native Americans and non-Native Americans honored Chief Joseph for his peaceful conduct and military skill. Mostly, Chief Joseph is remembered for his ability to speak about the common humanity of all peoples.

Little Bighorn, Battle of

Battle between the **Sioux** (see Vol. 1, p. 46) and the U.S. Seventh Cavalry Regiment. This battle took place in Montana Territory on the Little Bighorn River on June 25, 1876. **Sitting Bull** (see p. 47) and **Crazy Horse** (see p. 31) led the Sioux. The **Cheyenne** (see Vol. 1, p. 26) and **Arapaho** (see Vol. 1, p. 23) aided them. They had gone to war to protect their sacred region called the Black Hills from gold miners. As part of this conflict over the Black Hills, Lieutenant Colonel George Armstrong Custer led an attack against the Sioux

Little Bighorn

The Battle of Little Bighorn, between Lieutenant Colonel George Armstrong Custer's out-manned Seventh Calvary and the Sioux, occurred on June 25, 1876. Resulting in the deaths of over 200 soldiers, including Custer, and dozens of Sioux, it was one of the most grisly of U.S.–Native American encounters. This report from the July 7, 1876, *Bozeman Avant Courier* of Bozeman, Montana, details the fighting and its carnage.

The whole force of the command was twelve companies of the Seventh Cavalry. At the head of the five companies Custer charged the center of the sioux village from the north side of the Little Horn. The attack was made about three o'clock in the afternoon and lasted about three hours. Custer and his whole command, including sixteen officers, were killed. Two hundred and three dead bodies were found, among them was the whole Custer family, lying close together — the General, his two brothers, a brother-in-law and a nephew. Many of the men were horribly mutilated. Some had their heads cut off, some had their legs amputated at the hip joint; some were cut in strips. There were found on the battle ground fifty or sixty dead Indians — nine of whom were chiefs; men of distinguished note, as was evidenced by the fact that horses had been sacrificed to their names.

Source: *Bozeman Avant Courier*, 1876

on the Little Bighorn River. Custer and all his troops were killed. The defeat became known as "Custer's Last Stand."

Manifest Destiny

Belief in a divine plan for the United States to expand across the continent. John L. Sullivan first used the phrase "Manifest Destiny" in 1845. He was the editor of the *United States Magazine and Democratic Review*. His idea in using this phrase was that U.S. civilization was superior to that of the Native Americans and Mexicans. It was believed that God plainly (or "manifestly") intended for the United States to expand into those faraway places. This would provide room for its own people and spread the blessings of democracy and free enterprise. The idea of Manifest Destiny was used to justify the U.S. claims on areas held by Mexico and by Native Americans.

Meeker Massacre

Military encounter in 1879 between the U.S. and **Ute** (see Vol. 1, p. 47). During the 1870s, the Ute had given up or sold much of their land in Colorado and Utah. Settlers in Colorado tried to have the Ute removed from the territory. Indian agent Nathan Meeker tried to convert the Ute to non-Native American ways. He worked to convince the Ute to become farmers.

The Ute resisted and Meeker looked to the army for protection. A battle took place than involved hundreds of U.S. cavalry and infantry and Ute warriors. The U.S. drove the Ute into the Utah hills. In the fighting, Meeker was killed. This series of fighting and battles was known as the Ute War.

Mexican-American War

Military conflict between the United States and Mexico from 1846 to 1848. There were tensions between the U.S. and Mexico over the independent republic of Texas. In 1845, the United States took control of Texas. The United States and Mexico also disagreed about the southern boundary of Texas. In addition, the United States wanted the Mexican territories of New Mexico and California. The disagreements became reasons for war. In 1846, Mexican troops attacked U.S. forces in a Texas territory on the Rio Grande. Later, U.S. forces conquered New Mexico and

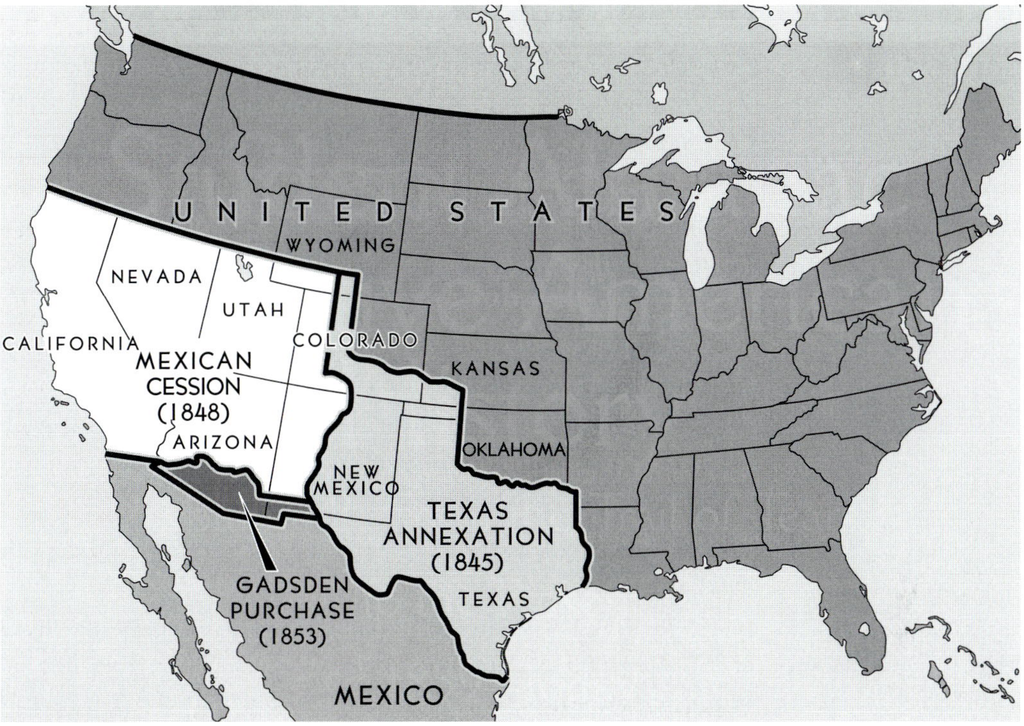

Between 1845 and 1853, the United States seized a vast amount of Mexico's northern territories. First, the United States annexed Texas, which had won its independence a few years earlier. Then, following victory over Mexico in the Mexican-American War, the United States gained control over California, Nevada, Utah, and much of what is now Colorado, Arizona, and New Mexico. Finally, in 1853, the United States purchased a strip of land in what is now southern Arizona and New Mexico. Each time U.S. territory grew, more Native American peoples came under the control of the U.S. government.

California. In 1847, General Winfield Scott captured Mexico City and Mexico surrendered. The Treaty of Guadalupe Hidalgo (*hid-AHL-go*) was signed in 1848. Under the treaty, Mexico gave up its claim to Texas, accepted the Rio Grande boundary, and gave up a vast region to the United States. This was called the Mexican Cession. It included what is now California, Nevada, and Utah, along with most of Arizona and New Mexico. In return, Mexico received $15 million. Mexico was also excused from paying $3 million in unpaid claims of U.S. citizens against Mexico.

The United States now governed the Mexicans and Native Americans living in the Mexican Cession. This included the **Pueblo** Indians (see Vol. 1, p. 44), who lived in settled towns in New Mexico. While the war was still going on, the Tiwa of Taos **Pueblo** (see Vol. 1, p. 44) revolted against the U.S. They killed the governor of New Mexico before U.S. forces ended the rebellion.

The **Navajo** (see Vol. 1, p. 41) and **Apache** (see Vol. 1, p. 22) also rebelled. They were ***nomads*** who hunted and herded animals. They also raided settled peoples. The Navajo and Apache resisted U.S. rule from 1846 to 1886. In the Treaty of Guadalupe Hidalgo, the United States became responsible for preventing Navajo and Apache raids into Mexico.

Modoc *(MO-dock)* War

Military conflict between **Modoc** (see Vol. 1, p. 39) people and U.S. forces. In 1864, the Modoc signed a treaty giving their lands to the United States. They also agreed to live on the Klamath (*KLAM-uth*) **Reservation** (see p. 45) in Oregon. Modoc chief Kintpuash (*kint-POO-ash*) was one of many who were dissatisfied with reservation conditions. He led a group of Modoc back to their ancestral lands on the Lost River in California. U.S. troops tried to force them out. For several months, the group of 250 Modoc held off a force of more than 1,000 soldiers. During an attempted peace conference, Kintpuash killed two members of the peace commission. The United States reacted with increased force, and the Modoc were defeated. Kintpuash and three others were hanged. The remaining Modoc were sent to reservations in Oklahoma.

Navajo War

Military conflict between the **Navajo** (see Vol. 1, p. 41) people and U.S. forces that took place between 1863 and 1866. The Navajo raided U.S. settlements from the time that the United States took possession of their territories in New Mexico and Arizona. To enforce a treaty and relocate the Navajo to a reservation, the U.S. Army and scout **Christopher "Kit" Carson** (see p. 25) began actions against the Navajo. Carson was ordered to carry out a "scorched earth" action. It was hoped that by destroying their land and their traditional way of life, the Navajo would be driven from their lands. Carson and his troop of volunteers took the Navajo livestock and burned their crops and all forms of plant life. They cornered the starving Navajo at the Canyon de Chelly in New Mexico.

After some resistance, 8,000 Navajo surrendered. They made the 300-mile "Long Walk" across New Mexico to the reservation at the Bosque Redondo on the Pecos River. It was the largest surrender in the Indian Wars. On the walk, many died from sickness. Others were shot by the U.S. military for being unable to continue the walk. At Bosque Redondo even more died from illness. A group of Navajo under leader Manuelito (*man-wel-EET-oh*) remained uncaptured. He later surrendered and went on to serve as Navajo chief.

In 1868, the U.S. and the Navajo signed a treaty. The Navajo were granted a better reservation in their homeland of the Chuska Mountains.

Nez Percé War

Military conflict in 1877 between the United States and the **Nez Percé** (see Vol. 1, p. 41). The U.S. government ordered the Lower Nez Percé, a band of the Nez Percé Nation, to leave their traditional homeland. It was in the Wallowa Valley of northeastern Oregon. They were to go to a reservation in Idaho. At first, the ***band***'s leader, **Chief Joseph** (see p. 36), agreed to leave. He thought the move would avoid war. When some of his warriors killed some settlers, war broke out. The Nez Percé defeated U.S. forces at White Bird Canyon, Idaho. Then they began a long journey toward Canada. They hoped to find new land there.

Their journey to Canada became known as the "Flight of the Nez Percé." They traveled about 1,000 miles. The band began in Idaho and went through Yellowstone Park in Wyoming all the way to northern Montana. Along the way, they fought against enemy forces for more than three months. Other Nez Percé bands joined them, until the group numbered about 700. Finally, in a five-day battle, U.S. forces under General Nelson Miles defeated them near the Bear Paw Mountains, just south of Canada. The Nez Percé were forced to move to Oklahoma. Later they were allowed to return to a reservation in Washington.

Parker, Ely Samuel

American military leader and government worker. Parker was a Seneca and was born in New York. He was trained as a lawyer at western New York colleges. He became a Seneca chief and helped the Seneca gain land rights for a reservation in New York.

Parker joined the Union army during the **Civil War** (see p. 27). He was a staff officer and became a military secretary to

General Ulysses S. Grant. Parker helped prepare the final surrender papers for the Confederate Army at Appomattox Courthouse. At the end of the war, he was named a brigadier general.

In 1869, President Grant named him as the commissioner of **Indian Affairs** (see Vol. 1, p. 104). He was the first Native American given this role.

Parker, Quanah

Quanah Parker
(Library of Congress)

Comanche (see Vol. 1, p. 29) chief. Quanah Parker was born in Texas. He was the son of Comanche chief Peta Nocona. In the Red River War, Quanah led a group of Comanche, **Kiowa** (see Vol. 1, p. 36), **Cheyenne** (see Vol. 1, p. 26), and **Arapaho** (see Vol. 1, p. 23) against settlers in Texas, Kansas, Colorado, and New Mexico. The war was sparked by the hunting of **buffalo** (see p. 22) by non-Native Americans. Quanah surrendered in 1875. Afterward, he and his band moved to a reservation near Fort Sill, Oklahoma. He remained a leader in peace as he had been in war. He helped his people learn to farm their land. He also got them full U.S. citizenship before most other Native Americans. After 1890, he was a founder of the peyote religion. It was named for the religious use of peyote. Peyote is a kind of cactus that can cause hallucinations that Native Americans believe to be spiritual visions. The use of peyote was a practice that had long been common in the Southwest and Mexico.

Peace Policy

Plan for dealing with Native Americans under President Ulysses S. Grant (1869-1877). President Grant wanted to end the Indian Wars. In 1870, he put into action a plan that became known as the Peace Policy. Under the Peace Policy, churches would take over running the **reservations** (see p. 45). Grant believed that this change would help settle the unrest among Native Americans. Before the Peace Policy, people who took advantage of the Native Americans ran the reservations. The military was also involved in settling problems on the reservations. With the Peace Policy, army officers were no longer allowed to be Indian agents. Church members ran the reservations. The policy was unable to stop warfare between Native Americans and settlers. Church-run reservations still relied on the military for help. In

Grant's Peace Policy

In 1870, President Ulysses S. Grant placed control of Indian agencies in the hands of Christian denominations that he hoped could "civilize" the Indian. This step followed a law prohibiting army officers from becoming Indian agents. President Grant discussed his peace policy in his Second Annual Message to Congress.

I determined to give all the [Indian] agencies to such religious denominations as had heretofore established missionaries among the Indians, and perhaps to some other denominations who would undertake to work on the same terms — i.e., as a missionary work. The societies selected are allowed to name their own agents, subject to [my] approval, and are expected to watch over them and aid them as missionaries, to Christianize and civilize the Indian, and to train him in the arts of peace. I ... hope that the policy now pursued will in a few years bring all the Indians upon reservations, where they will live in houses and have schoolhouses and churches, and will be pursuing peaceful and self-sustained avocations, and where they may be visited by the law-abiding white man with the same impunity that he now visits the civilized white settlements...."

Source: National Archives

addition, the churches tried to convert the Native Americans to Christianity. The Native American religions and cultures were being ignored. This meant that the Native Americans had less freedom than before. The Peace Policy was dropped under the term of the next president, Rutherford B. Hayes.

Powell, John Wesley

Geologist, explorer, and ***ethnologist.*** Powell was born in New York in 1834. He developed his interest in the west as he explored the Green and Colorado rivers. He was a pioneer in Native American ethnology, or the study of cultures. Powell published his book, *An Introduction to the Study of Indian Languages*, in 1877. The book was the first attempt to classify Native American languages.

In 1879, Powell became the first director of the Smithsonian Institution's Bureau of Ethnology, which studied the cultures of Native Americans. He also helped begin the U.S. Geological Survey. Other books by Powell include *Explorations of the Colorado River of the West and Its Tributaries* (1875) and *Report of the Arid Region of the United States* (1878). Powell died in 1904.

Pyramid Lake War

Military encounter in Nevada between the U.S. and Southern **Paiute** (see Vol. 1, p. 42) in 1860. The Pyramid Lake War was also known as the Paiute War. In the early 1860s, U.S. traders and Native Americans along the California Trail in modern-day Nevada began fighting. A force of 800 troops from California and Nevada met and fought the Paiute. The U.S. took the battle into the Pinnacle Mountains, where many Paiute fled. The Pyramid Lake War was the last large battle between the U.S. and Native Americans in the West before the **Civil War** (see p. 27).

Red Cloud's War

Red Cloud
(National Archives)

Military conflict from 1866 to 1868 between the United States and the **Sioux** (see Vol. 1, p. 46) and Northern **Cheyenne** (see Vol. 1, p. 26). Red Cloud's War was one of the few major clashes that ended in Native American victory. In 1863, John Bozeman opened a passage called the Bozeman Trail. The trail linked Fort Laramie, Wyoming, and Virginia City, Montana. The route ran through the hunting grounds of the Oglala Sioux. Red Cloud, an Oglala chief, refused to allow use of the trail. In 1866, the federal government responded by building forts along the trail. These were Fort Phil Kearny and Fort Reno in Wyoming and Fort C. F. Smith in Montana. Red Cloud attacked the forts for almost two years. These attacks made the trail impossible to use. In 1868, the United States recognized the Sioux claim to the land and left the forts. The Bozeman Trail came back into use in 1877.

Red River War

Military conflict between the United States and an alliance of **Comanche** (see Vol. 1, p. 29), **Kiowa** (see Vol. 1, p. 36), **Cheyenne** (see Vol. 1, p. 26), and **Arapaho** (see Vol. 1, p. 23). The Red River War, which took place in 1874 and 1875, was also known as the Buffalo War. Non-Native American hunters in the Great Plains region had been killing **buffalo** (see p. 22) in huge numbers. They killed the buffalo to sell the hides and make money. The Native Americans, who depended on buffalo for food, clothing, and tools, saw them being destroyed. Comanche chief **Quanah Parker** (see p. 42) formed an alliance of Native Americans to make war on the non-Native Americans in Texas, Kansas, Colorado, and New

Mexico. Troops led by generals Philip H. Sheridan, Ronald Mackenzie, and Nelson Miles battled with the Native Americans. By 1875, the last members of the alliance had surrendered. But by then, the buffalo population had been dramatically reduced.

reservations
Tracts of land set apart for use by Native Americans. The idea of "Indian reservations" had begun in colonial times. The more modern reservation system started in the 1850s. The use of reservations became widespread in the West after the **Civil War** (see p. 27). Most treaties with Native Americans required that they move to a tract of land set aside as a reservation. Reservations were sometimes located within their native homeland. However, often, it was in a different region altogether. Many western Native Americans were forced to move to reservations in **Indian Territory** (see Vol. 1, p. 106), now Oklahoma. This territory had been used for Native Americans as early as 1825. It was crowded with eastern Native American nations that had been forced to move there in the 1830s. The reservations in Indian Territory were promised as a permanent home for the people who moved there. These promises were often broken. Reservations were reduced to make room for railroads and settlers. The 1887 Allotment Policy Act (see **allotment policy**, p. 19) ended many reservations. The federal government put into action a plan to divide reservations into individual plots, or allotments. By 1907, Oklahoma

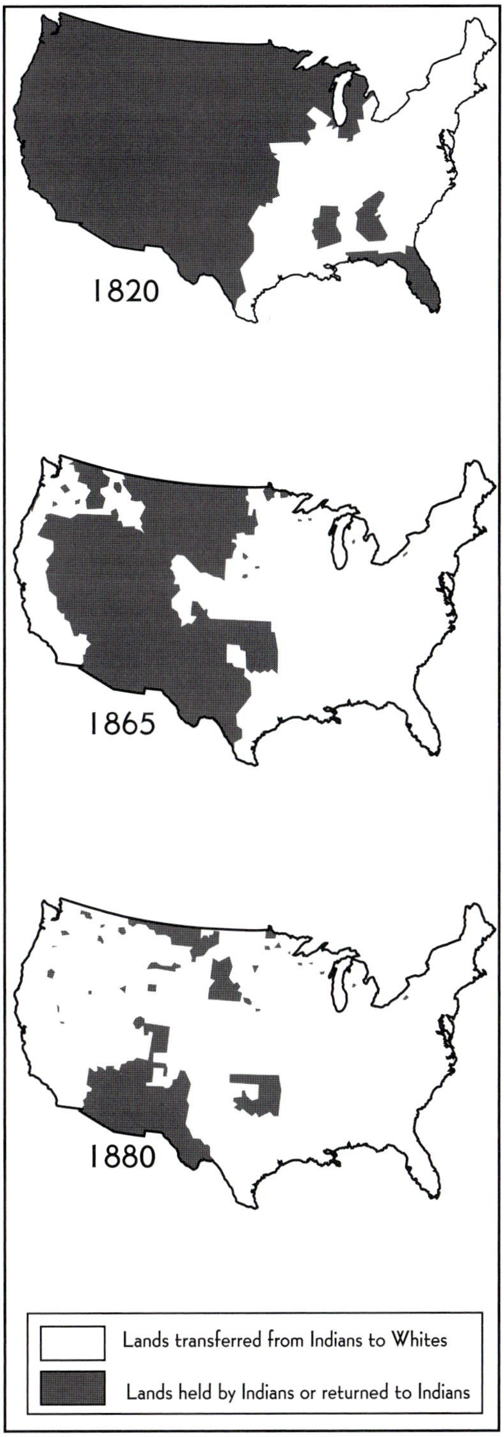

During the 19th century, Native Americans lost more and more of their lands to American settlers. The maps above show how Native Americans living west of the Mississippi River were left with mostly reservation land by 1880.

became a state. Its reservations were gone, though some other reservations survived elsewhere.

Reservations were typically in dry and barren places that were hard to farm. This was especially difficult for Plains Native Americans and others who had no farming experience. As a result, many Native Americans became totally dependent on government support. Some treaties that put them on reservations promised annuities, or annual payments. This support sometimes came in the form of food, supplies, or money. Agents who ran the reservations gave the support and payments to the Native Americans. These agents worked for the **Bureau of Indian Affairs** (see Vol. 1, p. 104). Many agents were ex-military officers accustomed to seeing Native Americans as enemies. They treated the Native Americans on the reservations unfairly and with harsh punishments.

President Ulysses S. Grant's **Peace Policy** (see p. 42) tried to change conditions on the reservations. It placed churches in charge of the reservations. This added a new problem to the reservations. Missionaries tried to change the Native Americans' religion and culture. The Peace Policy was soon dropped.

In the 19th century, reservations were guarded by the military. The military was there to prevent Native Americans from escaping and possibly harming settlers. Those who escaped, such as the **Nez Percé** (see Vol. 1, p. 41) in 1877 and the Northern **Cheyenne** (see Vol. 1, p. 26) in 1878-1879, were usually found and returned. This practice made 19th-century reservations seem like prison camps with a life that meant little food and much disease.

Reservations still exist today. They also still suffer from social problems. But many are also places where Native American governments, with federal help, have made great strides. These tribal governments have begun to improve the conditions of their people and to work to preserve their heritages.

Santee Uprising

Rebellion of the Santee **Sioux** (see Vol. 1, p. 46) in Minnesota and the Dakotas. The Santee Uprising is also known as the Minnesota Uprising. In 1851, Santee Sioux chief Little Crow gave most of his people's land to the United States. The settlers who moved into that territory mistreated the Sioux. The federal government also

During the Santee Uprising of 1862, Santee Sioux attacked white villages and killed settlers in Minnesota and the Dakotas after the U.S. government failed to live up to a treaty. In this photograph, white settlers in Minnesota are shown after having fled to safety. (Minnesota Historical Society)

failed to keep its treaty promises. In 1862, the Santee rebelled by attacking farms and killing settlers. Local forces and federal troops under General Henry Hastings Sibley ended the rebellion. In a single mass execution, the captured Santee Native Americans were hanged. Other members of the defeated Native American groups fled to Canada or joined the Teton Sioux in the Dakotas.

Seattle

Chief of the Duwamish-Suquamish (*doo-WAH-mish soo-KWA-mish*) people. Chief Seattle was born near present-day Seattle, Washington, in about 1786. He was a warrior during his youth. He was converted to Christianity and traded with the Hudson Bay Company. Chief Seattle believed in trying to have peaceful relations with settlers. In 1852, city founders named the city of Seattle after him. By 1854, the U.S. government forced him and his people off their land in Washington Territory. In a speech explaining his position, he said: "How can you buy or sell the sky? The land? The earth does not belong to man, man belongs to the earth." Chief Seattle died in 1866.

Chief Seattle
(Smithsonian Institution)

Sitting Bull

Lakota **Sioux** (see Vol. 1, p. 46) leader and medicine man. Sitting Bull was born in South Dakota in 1834. He was known from his

Sitting Bull (Library of Congress)

youth as a warrior. Sitting Bull became a chief of the Northern Sioux in 1866. He tried to make peace with the U.S. government. However, when gold was discovered in the Black Hills, miners and settlers moved onto Sioux lands. Sitting Bull became the leader of the Sioux war council. He led his people in the Sioux War for the Black Hills. He also planned the attack against Lieutenant Colonel George Armstrong Custer and the U.S. cavalry at the **Battle of Little Bighorn** (see p. 37). Afterward, he tried to settle in Canada. The Canadian government did not allow him permission to move his people there. He returned to the U.S. and was placed on a **reservation** (see p. 45).

In 1885 and 1886, Sitting Bull appeared in Buffalo Bill Cody's Wild West Show (see **western entertainment**, p. 52). He also became active in the **Ghost Dance religion** (see p. 34). This was a religion

The Journey of Standing Bear

In 1877, Ponca chief Standing Bear and his people were forced to evacuate their Nebraska homeland and travel hundreds of miles to a reservation. Later, Standing Bear informed a reporter about the trip. His description resulted in a public outcry, a Senate investigation, and a ruling to allow some of the Ponca to return home. In "Standing Bear's Odyssey," the chief recalls the journey and its costs.

They took everything we had on our farms. Then they put into the wagons such things as they could carry. We told them that we would rather die than leave our lands; but we could not help ourselves. They took us down. Many died on the road. Two of my children died.... After we reached the new land all my horses died. The water was very bad. All our cattle died. I stayed till one hundred fifty-eight of my people had died. Then I ran away with thirty of my people. When we reached the Omaha Reserve the Omahas gave us a piece of land, and we were in a hurry to plough it and put in wheat. While we were working, the soldiers came and arrested us. Half of us were sick. We would rather have died than have been carried back; but we could not help ourselves.

Source: Peter Nabokov, ed., *Native American Testimony*

that promised a time when the earth would be restored to Native Americans. Native American police killed Sitting Bull in 1890.

Standing Bear

Ponca chief. In the 19th century, the Ponca Nation had migrated from its original location in Dakota Territory to as far south as the Missouri River. A congressional act was passed to relocate the Poncas from Nebraska to **Indian Territory** (see Vol. 1, p. 106). Shortly after the act's passage, Standing Bear's son died. The chief tried to return to his ancestral land for his son's burial. On his journey, he was arrested and put into prison by U.S. troops.

The government brought him to trial and claimed that Native Americans were not considered persons under the U.S. Constitution. Judge Elmer S. Dundy ruled for the Poncas. He said they were to be granted rights as persons under the law. Standing Bear was permitted to bury his son on ancestral ground. He and some of his people were permitted to return to their former home

The End of Treaty Making

In 1871, Congress decided that it would no longer recognize any group of Native Americans as "an independent nation, tribe, or power with whom the United States may contract by treaty." This brought an end to the making of U.S.-Indian treaties, after about 370 such documents had been ratified. In taking this step, Congress heeded the advice of the commissioner of Indian Affairs, who had made the following recommendation in a report to Congress two years earlier.

A treaty involves the idea of a compact between two or more sovereign powers, each possessing sufficient authority and force to compel a compliance with the obligations incurred. The Indian tribes of the United States are not sovereign nations, capable of making treaties, as none of them have an organized government of such inherent strength as would secure a faithful obedience of its people in the observance of compacts of this character. But because treaties have been made with them, generally for the extinguishments of their supposed absolute title to the land inhabited by them, they have become falsely impressed with the notion of national independence. It is time that this idea should be dispelled, and the government ceases this cruel farce of thus dealing with its helpless and ignorant wards.

Source: Library of Congress

in Nebraska. Judge Dundy's ruling became a landmark decision for Native American rights.

Supreme Court decisions

Rulings of the nation's highest court. The 19th-century wars between Native Americans and non-Native Americans were fought in courts as well as on battlefields. Several Supreme Court decisions from 1839 to 1890 affected the status of Native Americans.

In a case called *The Kansas Indians*, three Native American nations in Kansas tried to stop Indian lands from being sold for nonpayment of state taxes. The three nations were the **Shawnee** (see Vol. 1, p. 45), Wea, and **Miami** (see Vol. 1 p. 38). The Supreme Court ruled in their favor. It argued that Native American nations and their members, living on reservations, could not be taxed by states. Native Americans living within tribal organizations were "to be governed exclusively by the federal government." This ruling protected Native Americans from state control. However, federal control increased as Native American power was reduced. The practice of making treaties with Native Americans came to an end in 1871. At this time, Native American nations were no longer considered sovereign nations.

In 1885, Congress passed the Major Crimes Act. This act gave the federal government control over seven crimes, including murder, if they took place on reservations. In *United States* v. *Kagama* (*kuh-GAH-muh*) (1886), the Supreme Court ruled that the Major Crimes Act was constitutional. The court called Native Americans "wards of the nation" and "remnants of a race once powerful, now weak and diminished in numbers" who were in need of federal protection.

Even though Native Americans were under the control of federal rule, they had no citizenship rights. In *McKay* v. *Campbell* (1870), the Supreme Court ruled that Indians born in tribal allegiance were not citizens. Citizenship for Native Americans born in the United States would not come until Congress granted it in 1924.

Walla Walla Council

Meeting of Native Americans with Isaac Stevens in 1855. Stevens was the governor of Washington Territory. This council took place in the Walla Walla Valley in what is now Washington State. Stevens persuaded the **Nez Percé** (see Vol. 1, p. 41), Cayuse, Walla Walla, **Yakima** (see Vol. 1 p. 48), **Umatilla** (see Vol. 1, p. 47), and other Native American nations to give up most of their land. The Native American nations also agreed to move to a reservation. In exchange, they would receive payments and benefits, such as schools, homes, and livestock. They also received a promise that they would not have to move for at least two years. That promise was broken within days of the treaty signing. Stevens opened the Native American lands to settlement. The Native American nations reacted with violence. The result was a period of war. Two of these wars were the Yakima War, which involved the Yakima, Walla Walla, Cayuse, Umatilla, and other nations; and the Coeur d'Alene (*CORE-duh-layn*) War, involving the Coeur d'Alene, Spokan, Northern Paiute, and Palouse, among others.

At the Walla Walla Council of 1855, several Native American nations agreed to surrender their land in exchange for a promise that they would receive payments and benefits. Although the government of Washington Territory agreed that it would not force the native peoples to move again for at least two years, the treaty was broken by white settlers in only a few days. This illustration shows Native Americans from a number of nations arriving at the council. (Library of Congress)

Watie, Stand

Cherokee leader and Confederate soldier. Stand was born in Georgia in 1806. He believed in the removal of his people to Indian Territory and signed the Treaty of New Echota (*eck-OH-tuh*). This treaty called for that removal. In 1861, when the Civil War broke out, he formed an alliance between the Cherokee and the Confederacy. Stand organized and led a volunteer Cherokee regiment. It was called the First Cherokee Mounted Rifles. The regiment saw action in the Battle of Pea Ridge, Arkansas. He became the only Native American brigadier general in the Confederacy and was the last Confederate general to surrender. He died in 1871.

western entertainment

The 19th-century conflicts between Native Americans and non-Native Americans in the West were not over when they became the subject of popular entertainment. Stories of capture continued, as they had since the 17th century. These firsthand accounts of settlers captured by Native Americans were usually filled with stories of violence. In addition, a new type of literature became famous. It was the western. These were novels about gunplay and adventure on the frontier. Native Americans were almost always portrayed as bloodthirsty villains who murdered innocent settlers. American cowboys were the heroes. Like other books, westerns were often priced at ten cents and known as dime novels.

Western writers included Edward Wheeler, who created the hero character Deadwood Dick. Edward Judson wrote under the name Ned Buntline. Judson made real-life frontier scout William F. Cody famous as Buffalo Bill. Buffalo Bill was the hero of a series of novels starting with *Buffalo Bill, the King of the Border Men.* Cody himself began another form of western entertainment with his traveling Wild West Show. The show supposedly portrayed life on the Great Plains. It began in 1883 and toured for nearly 20 years. For a time it featured real-life Sioux chief **Sitting Bull** (see p. 47). Like the dime novels, Buffalo Bill's Wild West Show presented Native Americans as fearsome killers. The injustices that caused Native Americans to go to war were rarely portrayed. The image of Native Americans as violent warriors remained in westerns in the next century. Then, the same image of Native Americans moved to western stories on film and television. In

This historic poster advertises Buffalo Bill's Wild West Show. Buffalo Bill can be seen on the right of the poster. (Library of Congress)

Eyewitness at Wounded Knee

John Little Finger was a Miniconjou Lakota Sioux who was wounded in the massacre of his people at Wounded Knee, South Dakota, on December 29, 1890. To try to escape the bullets of the U.S. Seventh Cavalry, he hid with others in a deep gorge, or ravine. He found that there was no safety either there or on the flat plain above.

In this ravine where we took refuge, most of them were women and children and, of course, defenseless and helpless; above them the soldiers just got near them and shot these people down. This was kept up until I heard a voice, an Indian voice, calling from some place in a very far distance, saying that these Indians were to come out of there because fighting was not to be continued. So some of these, not yet killed, left the big ravine of refuge, and they went up on the flat. I was not with them, because I was shot through in two places, one through my leg and my foot. So I crawled along until I got over where those that were ahead of me sat in a circle up there, and the soldiers were surrounding them. I got up on the flat, a little distance from them, and they started to shoot them again and killing them. Of course those that were not shot tried to get away.

Source: James McGregor, *The Wounded Knee Massacre: From the Viewpoint of the Sioux*

recent years, film and television producers have tried to present a more balanced view of Native American life.

Wounded Knee Massacre

Military encounter between U.S. Seventh Cavalry Division and the Sioux. In 1890, the U.S. banned the practice of the **Ghost Dance religion** (see p. 34) on Native American reservations. This religion said that the earth would soon be restored to Native Americans. When a group of Sioux kept practicing the religion, U.S. forces tried to stop them at Wounded Knee, South Dakota. In the confusion that followed, at least 150 Sioux adults and children were killed. This was the final event in the Sioux Wars. It was also the final major military encounter between U.S. forces and Native Americans.

CHAPTER TWO

Exiled at Home

The Reservation and World Wars, 1891–1945

"[W]e Native Americans will be Native Americans all our lives, we will never be white men. We can talk and work and go to school like the white people, but we're still Native Americans."

—Olney Runs After, an elderly Native American, in the 1970s, recalling a prediction from 1912 that Native Americans would cease to exist within 40 years

The peace that followed the end of the Indian Wars was nearly as deadly for Native Americans as armed conflict had been. In the U.S. ***Census*** of 1900, the Native American population reached an all-time low of 237,196. This was a fraction of the millions who existed before Europeans arrived. Many non-Native Americans considered Native Americans to be a dying people or "vanishing race." Even those who wanted to help Native Americans believed that their only hope was to blend into the larger society. But something surprising happened in the 20th century. Native Americans did not vanish, and they did not completely blend into society. They survived as a distinct people.

The Indian Wars left Native Americans poor—probably the poorest people in the country. Their only major possession was the land they had been granted in treaties and agreements. These lands were either in **Indian Territory** (see Vol. 1, p. 106) or in **reservations** (see p. 45) across the nation. On these lands, they lived largely as dependents on federal aid. The aid was often scarce and filled with bureaucratic rules. Yet, even their land was being chipped away. On April 29, 1889, the federal government opened a large part of Indian Territory to settlement by non-Native Americans. About 50,000 settlers arrived on that day alone. In 1890, the land carved out of Indian Territory became the

Territory of **Oklahoma** (see p. 81). Native American holdings in the region kept shrinking. The non-Native American population boomed. By 1907, when Oklahoma achieved statehood and Indian Territory ceased to exist, Native Americans made up less than 10 percent of the new state's population.

Native American lands outside Indian Territory were also being broken up. Ever since Congress passed the General Allotment Act in 1887 (see **allotment policy**, p. 19), federal policy was to distribute, or allot, shares of tribal land to individual Native American heads of household. Each individual plot was to be 160 acres, with surplus lands sold to whites. The hope was to encourage Native Americans to blend into society by replacing tribal ownership with individual ownership. But the effect was a decreased amount of land held by Native Americans. Many Native Americans were easily bullied or cheated out of their holdings by non-Native American land speculators.

Loss of land through allotment did not take place all at once. Until the mid-1890s, relatively few reservations were split up. As new western states joined the Union, they sent representatives to Washington. The representatives put pressure on Congress to speed up the allotment process. Court decisions and new acts of Congress did just that. The **Supreme Court decision** (see p. 85 and sidebar, p. 82) of *Lone Wolf* v. *Hitchcock* (1903) allowed Congress to set aside the details of any Native American treaty. These included forbidding the sale of Native American lands. The **Curtis Act** of 1898 (see p. 72) abolished tribal governments in Indian Territory. This permitted allotment to proceed there.

Timeline

1891

The Indian Schools Act promotes the building of schools based on the Carlisle Indian School in Pennsylvania. **Boarding schools** such as Carlisle separate Native American children from their families to promote **assimilation**.

1898

The **Curtis Act** abolishes Native American governments in **Indian Territory**. This permits **allotment** or distribution of Native American land to individual owners.

The **Burke Act** (see p. 69) of 1906 allowed individual Native Americans to be entrusted with complete ownership of their lands earlier than before—and sell it just as fast.

In Oklahoma, some Native Americans resisted allotment through acts of resistance and civil disobedience. These took the form of nonviolent refusal to obey laws. Redbirth Smith of the Cherokee and Chitto Harjo (*CHIT-toe HAR-jo*) of the Creek both led movements in which they refused to accept allotments. They also refused to enroll as tribal members in preparation for allotment. They encouraged their fellow Native Americans to keep their traditional customs and the old treaties in which the United States had granted land to their nations. Harjo's Crazy Snake Uprising was crushed by federal officials and U.S. cavalry in 1901, and Smith was arrested and forced to enroll in 1902.

By 1920, Native American reservations were the site of numerous activities by non-Native Americans, including farming, ranching, logging, and mining. These were carried out on land bought or leased from the Native Americans. By 1934, Native Americans had lost about two-thirds of the land they had held before the allotment policy started.

The culture of Native Americans was also under assault. In 1879, the Carlisle Indian School was founded at a former military post in Pennsylvania. Its goal was to "civilize" Native American children. The children were separated from their families and required to give up native customs. They had to wear non-Native American clothing, give up their native languages, and learn trades

1900

The Native American population of the United States reaches its all-time low, 237,196 in this year's U.S. Census.

1901

In the Crazy Snake Uprising in **Oklahoma**, Chitto Harjo, a Creek, leads an armed resistance movement against the allotment process. Federal forces bring the uprising to an end.

1902

In **Oklahoma**, Cherokee resistance leader Redbird Smith is arrested and forced to participate in the allotment process, which he had been protesting.

1903

In *Lone Wolf* v. *Hitchcock*, the Supreme Court permits Congress to abrogate, or set aside, the provisions of any Native American treaty.

such as blacksmithing and sewing. The school became the model for a system of federally supported **boarding schools** (see p. 68). Many of the schools were located in the West. The federal superintendent of Native American schools said in 1885, "[W]e must recreate him [the Native American], make him a new personality." (See also **assimilation policy**, p. 67.)

On the reservations, many Native American religious ceremonies were prohibited, including the Sun Dance. The Sun Dance was a Great Plains ritual that involved self-torture and worship of the sun. The 1913 **Supreme Court decision** (see p. 85) in *U.S.* v. *Sandoval* (1913) weakened the ability of the Native American nations to regulate their own affairs. This decision permitted federal supervision of their religious beliefs and other ways of life.

Despite the push to have Native Americans blend into society, many resisted. Some parents hid children to prevent them from being taken to the schools. Some students ran away and returned home. Others stayed at the schools but grew up drifting between two cultures. They felt as if they belonged to neither culture. Native Americans secretly performed banned religious ceremonies. In the Southwest and Plains, a new **peyote religion** (see p. 83) began that blended Christianity with older Native American rituals. The religion involved the use of the mind-altering drug peyote. There were many efforts to ban peyote ceremonies. In 1918, Native Americans from many nations founded the Native American Church in Oklahoma. It was to be a safe haven for such practices.

1906

The **Burke Act** permits the federal government to change the trust period for allotted lands. This speeds the loss of Native American land through sale or lease to non-Native Americans.

1907

Oklahoma becomes a state, bringing an end to Indian Territory. It had once been promised as a permanent homeland for Native Americans.

1908

In *Winters v. United States*, the Supreme Court establishes the **Winters Doctrine**. It gives Native Americans the right to have enough water for agricultural uses on their reservations.

1911

The **Society of American Indians** is founded for reform of federal Native American policies. The same year, **Ishi**, of the Yahi Nation, arrives in a small California town. Scientists had thought the Yahi had become extinct.

Native Americans took other actions in the early 20th century to improve their ways of life and to defend their civil rights. They launched court battles and formed support groups. In *Winters* v. *United States* (1908), the Supreme Court established the **Winters Doctrine** (see p. 87). This ***doctrine*** gave Native Americans the right to have enough water for agricultural uses on their reservations. In Washington, D.C., in 1911, several prominent Native Americans founded the **Society of American Indians** (see p. 84). The society was formed to lobby the U.S. Congress for reform of federal Native American policies. In 1912, the **Alaska Native Brotherhood** (see p. 63) was founded to promote the voting rights and other civil liberties of Native Americans in Alaska.

Before the 20th century, non-Native Americans who had wanted to help Native Americans had usually encouraged them to blend into society and accept allotment. One example was the **Friends of the Indian** (see p. 73) movement. This group met once a year at Lake Mohonk, New York. But even non-Native Americans became more aware of the problems with federal policy. John Collier founded the **American Indian Defense Association** (see p. 63) in 1923. Collier spoke against allotment and tried to defend Native American freedoms. Anthropologists Franz Boas and Alfred Kroeber spread a new understanding of and respect for Native American cultures. Books such as **Charles Eastman**'s (see p. 72) *Indian Heroes and Great Chieftains* (1925) and the autobiography *My People the Sioux* (1928) by Luther Standing Bear helped to bring Native American issues to a wider audience (see **arts and entertainment**, p. 64).

1912

Athlete **Jim Thorpe** of the Sac and Fox Nations wins Olympic gold medals for the pentathlon and decathlon. They are taken away in 1913, in a controversy over his amateur status, but reinstated in 1984.

1912

The **Alaska Native Brotherhood** is founded to advance the civil rights of Native Americans in Alaska.

1913

In *U.S. v. Sandoval*, the Supreme Court permits federal supervision of any communities regarded as "distinctly Indian."

1914

Native American activist **Carlos Montezuma** releases his book, *Let My People Go.*

On many fronts, non–Native Americans began to look more with sympathy on Native Americans. Native American athletes began to impress sports audiences. The most famous was **Jim Thorpe** (see p. 85). He won two Olympic gold medals in 1912. More than 8,000 Native Americans served in **World War I** (see p. 87). This fact helped convince Congress in 1924 to grant U.S. **citizenship** (see p. 70) to all Native Americans who did not already possess it. Native American populations showed the first signs of recovery. By 1920, the U.S. Census reported 244,437 Native Americans, about 7,000 more than in 1900.

Although some steps were taken by the federal government to improve the condition of Native Americans (see **Snyder Act**, p. 84), most Native Americans lived in very poor conditions. In 1928, a study of federal Native American policies was issued. It added fuel to the calls for reform. It was titled *The Problem of Indian Administration*. The private Brookings Institution issued it. The study was better known as the **Meriam Report** (see p. 78) for its lead author, Lewis Meriam. It found that most Native Americans were "poor, even extremely poor," that they suffered from many health problems, and that their diet, housing, sanitation, and schooling were all inadequate. It declared the **allotment policy** (see p. 19) a failure and urged Congress to spend more money to fulfill its obligations toward Native Americans.

The Meriam Report led to some reform during the presidency of Herbert Hoover (1929-1933). Some boarding schools were closed and community day

1918

The Native American Church, which practices the **peyote religion**, is founded in **Oklahoma**.

1922

In New Mexico, the Pueblo get public support to defeat the **Bursum bill**. The bill would have given land titles to non-Native American squatters on Pueblo lands.

1923

The **American Indian Defense Association** is founded to advance Native American rights. It calls for an end to allotment and protection of Native American cultural and religious freedoms.

1924

Congress passes the **Citizenship Act**, granting U.S. citizenship to all Native Americans who do not already possess it.

schools were established. Bigger changes came during the **New Deal** (see p. 79) presidency of Franklin D. Roosevelt (1933-1945). In the midst of the **Great Depression** (see p. 74), Roosevelt appointed reformer John Collier, founder of American Indian Defense Association, as commissioner of Indian Affairs.

In what became known as the "Indian New Deal," Collier increased assistance to Native Americans while showing a new respect for the value of tribal culture. In 1934, Collier won passage of the **Indian Reorganization Act** (IRA) (see p. 76). This act banned further allotment of tribal lands. It also encouraged nations to govern and provide for themselves. The law provided for purchase of new lands and restoration of surplus lands that had already been opened for sale. It permitted Native American nations to resume self-government under their own constitutions and bylaws. It funded economic development through tribal business corporations and ***vocational*** training.

Other reforms began with Collier's work. The **Johnson-O'Malley Act** (see p. 78) of 1934 allowed the federal government to contract with states to provide educational, medical, and other social services for Native Americans. Native American religious freedom was guaranteed. Steps were taken to preserve Native American languages. The **Indian Arts and Crafts Board** (see p. 75) was established to promote traditional Native American crafts. Many Native Americans benefited from the economic help of New Deal programs. These included the Works Progress Administration (WPA) and the Civilian Conservation Corps (CCC).

1926

The **Indian Defense League** is founded to provide legal representation for poor Indians.

1928

The Brookings Institution issues the **Meriam Report**. The report is a study that criticizes federal Indian policies and exposes the poverty, ill health, poor education, and loss of land widely suffered by Native Americans.

1933–1945

Native Americans benefit from the administration of President Franklin D. Roosevelt. Native Americans receive more assistance and greater respect for their cultures. Many find jobs in programs such as the Works Progress Administration (WPA).

1934

The **Indian Reorganization Act** (IRA) ends federal allotment policy. It bans further allotment of Native American lands, provides for some land restoration, permits limited self-government, and offers loans for Native American business corporations and vocational training.

Not all Native Americans approved of Collier's work. Some wanted to abolish the **Bureau of Indian Affairs** (see Vol. 1, p. 104). They wanted complete control returned to Native Americans themselves. Even so, the Native American New Deal was a turning point in the struggle of Native Americans not to vanish, but survive and flourish.

The U.S. entry into **World War II** (see p. 88) in 1941 stopped reform efforts on the reservations. The U.S. turned its attention to war in Europe and the Pacific. The war brought new opportunities for Native Americans. More than 25,000 Native Americans served valiantly in the armed forces. They won many medals, including two Congressional Medals of Honor. The Navajo **Code Talkers** (see p. 71) used their native language to transmit coded messages and received special renown. The Pima **Ira Hamilton Hayes** (see p. 75) was one of the men who raised the American flag on Iwo Jima in 1945. Thousands of other Native Americans served in defense industries. This meant that many of them held jobs for the first time. There were also signs of a rising sense of **pan-Indianism** (see p. 114). This is a term that refers to unity among all Native Americans. One such sign was the formation in 1944 of the National Congress of American Indians. This was a new organization. It was formed to advance Native American rights and it represented 50 nations from across the United States. It pointed to a growing willingness among Native Americans to join together to improve their condition.

1934

The **Johnson-O'Malley Act** authorizes the federal government to contract with states to provide educational, medical, and other social services for Native Americans.

1936

The **Indian Arts and Crafts Board** is established to promote traditional Native American crafts.

1941-1945

More than 25,000 Native Americans serve in the armed forces in World War II, including the Navajo **Code Talkers**, who use their native language to send and receive coded messages.

1944

Representatives from 50 tribes found the **National Congress of American Indians**, an organization to advance Indian rights.

A-Z of Key People, Events, and Terms

Alaska Native Brotherhood

Native American organization in Alaska. It was founded in 1912 to promote and protect the civil rights of Alaskan Native Americans. The brotherhood began when the **Tlingit** (*TLIN-git*) (see Vol. 1, p. 47) resisted the movement of non-Native Americans into their territory. First came Russian fur traders in the 19th century. Later, the arrival of Americans in search of gold. The newcomers also wanted to develop the fishing industry. All brought hardships to the Native Americans. U.S. officials ignored the Tlingit's land claims. The U.S. Navy was used to prevent rebellion. Alcohol and disease also took their toll. In a struggle to save their traditions and rights, the Tlingit joined other Indian nations in creating the Alaska Native Brotherhood. A partner organization, the Alaska Native Sisterhood, was founded in 1915. The Alaska Native Brotherhood is one of the earliest of modern intertribal organizations. It remains active today.

American Indian Defense Association (AIDA)

Organization to protect Native American rights. John Collier founded the AIDA in 1923. Collier later led **New Deal** (see p. 79) efforts in support of Native Americans under President Franklin D. Roosevelt. AIDA valued American Indian culture, particularly its emphasis on community. The AIDA tried to protect Native American cultural and religious freedom. It called for an end to allotment of land. It also worked to save Native American nations' titles to remaining reservations. The organization fought for federal protection of Indian water rights and for improvements in healthcare and education. The Indian Reorganization Act (1934) included many of the AIDA goals. In 1937, AIDA joined with another organization to become the Association on American Indian Affairs.

arts and entertainment

Artistic works by Native Americans during the early 20th century were viewed in different ways. The U.S. government criticized some of them. Others were concerned that Native American art would be lost. Those who viewed works about Native Americans by others were fascinated. Still others felt a sense of urgency that the Native Americans were a vanishing breed.

Autobiographies were an important part of Native American literature. Experiences at government-run schools were the background for the 1900 autobiography *The Middle Five*. An Omaha, Francis La Flesche (*luh-FLESH*), wrote it. *Indian Boyhood* (1902), by Sioux writer **Charles Eastman** (see p. 72), explored similar subjects. Novels about the difficulties of blending into society include John Joseph Mathews's *Sundown* (1934) and D'Arcy (*DAHR-see*) McNickle's *The Surrounded* (1936). Important autobiographies of Native American leaders include Geronimo's *Story of His Life* (1906) and *Autobiography of Luther Standing Bear* (1928).

Other kinds of writing were also represented. For children, there was *Old Indian Legends*. This was written by Sioux writer Gertrude Bonnin (Zitkala-Sa) (*zit-kuh-luh-SA*). Letters were included in *Indian Journal* by Creek writer Alexander Posey. Called the "Fus Fixico (*fus fix-SEE-ko*) Letters," they were about the effects of **allotment policy** (see p. 19). Literature that drew upon a people's culture became popular. An example was *Myths and Legends of the Sioux* by Marie McLaughlin (1916).

The first known novel by a Native American is the 1899 work *Queen of the Woods*. It was written by Chief Simon Pokagon. Novels about the clash of cultures include Mourning Dove's *Co-ge-we-a (co-gee-WEE-uh), the Half Blood* (1927). The most popular Native American novelist of the 1920s was John Oskison (*ahs-KEE-sun*). His novels included *Wild Harvest* (1926).

In art, an important trend of the period was the development of Pueblo painters. Many of them worked with watercolors. They included Julian Martinez (*mar-TEEN-ez*), Abel Sanchez, Fred Kabotie (*kuh-BOW-tee*), and Crescenio (*cres-SEEN-ee-oh*) Martinez. In the 1920s, a group of painters combined modern art deco and traditional forms in their work. These artists were from

Oklahoma (see p. 81) and were called the "Kiowa Five." In 1941, Native American art received national critical attention at an exhibition at the Museum of Modern Art.

One of the few Native American filmmakers during the early years of film was a Winnebago, James Young Deer. He became head of production of the company Pathe in Los Angeles. Among the dozens of films he oversaw was *A Cheyenne Brave* (1910).

The best-known Native American entertainer of the era was part-Cherokee humorist Will Rogers. He was a headliner on stage in ***vaudeville*** and in the Ziegfeld Follies. He also appeared in films and had a national newspaper column that ran from 1922 until his death in 1935.

Will Rogers (Library of Congress)

The longest lasting play of the period by a Native American was "Green Grow the Lilacs." It was by Cherokee playwright Lynn Riggs. The play was about the settlement of **Oklahoma** (see p. 81) territory. It became the basis for the Rodgers and Hammerstein musical "Oklahoma!" in 1943.

Literary works about Native Americans were varied. From 1897 to 1930, Edward S. Curtis recorded 10,000 songs and took 40,000 photographs of people from 80 Native American nations throughout the West. He wanted to capture what he believed was a "vanishing race."

"As-told-to" autobiographies were also published. Native Americans, who did not write, dictated these autobiographies. Among them are the *Autobiography of a Fox-Woman* (1918), by Truman Michaelson; *The Autobiography of a Papago Woman*, by ***anthropologist*** Ruth Underhill; and *Black Elk Speaks* (1932), as told to John G. Neihardt.

Early representation of Native Americans in film by non-Native Americans included "The Sioux Ghost Dance." The Thomas A. Edison Company (1894) produced this film. It was the first-known motion picture about Native Americans. The film presented non-Native American actors dressed as warriors in

Edward S. Curtis photographed over 40,000 Native Americans in the early 1900s. This photograph of a young Navajo girl was taken in 1909. (Library of Congress)

loincloths and feather headdresses. Other similar films followed over the next decade. Likewise, silent films about real Native Americans became popular. Among the titles directed by D. W. Griffith is "The Redman and the Child" (1910). Producer Thomas Ince (*IN-see*) received government permission to bring Sioux from their reservation to appear in dozens of western films. It was uncommon for Native Americans to work with white filmmakers. Among these films was "The Indian Massacre" (1912). In 1913, Cecil B. DeMille's first feature-length western was titled "The Squaw Man." It starred Winnebago actress Redwing.

Tonto, the Native American companion of the masked western hero the Lone Ranger, was introduced in the movie serial "The Lone Ranger" (1938). Tonto was played by Cherokee chief Thunder Cloud. A radio series of the same name was popular during the 1930s and 1940s, as was a television show in the 1950s.

Native American music played a role in popular and classical creations. An example is Antonin Dvorak's (duh-VOR-jhak) "New World Symphony" (1895). The symphony used elements of the music of the Omaha people.

Native American government programs included the Seneca Arts Project. This was a **New Deal** (see p. 79) program that ran from 1934 to 1941. It resulted in the creation of over 5,000 works of traditional and nontraditional art.

assimilation policy

Government programs designed to control and educate Native Americans. Between 1890 and 1934, the government enacted laws that affected most parts of Native American life. These laws were attempts to move Native Americans into mainstream society and eliminate reservations. By 1890, the government had relocated Native Americans away from their communities and onto reservations. U.S. Indian agents controlled these sites. The agents controlled the ways in which Native Americans could make a living, educate their children, practice their government, and celebrate their beliefs.

Tom Toslino, a young Navajo, is shown before and after enrolling in an Indian school. (Library of Congress)

Over the next ten years, the government passed many laws that affected the ways of life of Native Americans. Several allotment acts divided Native American land among individual Native Americans. The Indian School Construction Act allowed the removal of Native American leaders. There were acts that banned Native American courts and Native American lawmaking. Other laws banned liquor in "Indian country." Those who resisted these laws were punished. An example was the imprisonment in 1895 of 19 Hopi men on Alcatraz Island in San Francisco Bay for refusing to send their children to boarding school.

By the mid-1930s, the **Indian Reorganization Act** (see p. 76) and the **Johnson-O'Malley Act** (see p. 78) were passed. These acts provided for the movement toward self-government and government land restoration for Native Americans.

boarding schools

Schools where children live away from home. Church groups had run boarding schools for Native Americans since colonial times. The goals of the church groups were to spread Christian teaching and to train **missionaries** (see Vol. 1, p. 70). However, many Native American boarding schools were founded in the late 19th and early 20th centuries without ties to churches. In these boarding schools, the government hoped to assimilate Native American children into non-Native American society.

The best-known model for these schools was the Carlisle Indian School, founded by **Richard Henry Pratt** (see p. 83) in Carlisle, Pennsylvania, in 1879. Pratt built the school at a former military post. His stated goal was "civilizing" Native American children. Other schools followed this model. Children were separated from their families and were required to wear non-Native American clothing. They were not allowed to speak their native languages or practice their native customs. Under what was called the "outing system," the children spent time living with and working for white families outside the school. The students received an academic education. However, the emphasis was on learning work skills such as blacksmithing for boys and sewing for girls.

The federal government used the Carlisle Indian School as a model. It soon began other schools in California, Oregon, New Mexico, Arizona, Nebraska, and **Oklahoma** (see p. 81). Some

Students at the Carlisle Indian School. (Library of Congress)

schools were privately funded or run by churches. Pratt believed in building schools far away from reservations. The government built them on or close to reservations. In any case, many students at boarding schools were unhappy. They were separated from their families and taught to reject their cultures and traditions. Many of their parents felt the same way.

In the early 20th century, people believed the boarding school system had become too expensive. They also thought that the schools had been unsuccessful in assimilating Native American children. In the 1930s, the federal government began educating Native American children in community day schools and public schools. The Carlisle school closed in 1918.

Burke Act

Federal law passed in 1906. In 1887, the General Allotment Act (see **allotment policy**, p. 19) ordered that tribal lands be divided into shares and given to individual Native Americans. The law added that the federal government would hold the allotted land in ***trust*** for 25 years. During that trust period, Native American landowners could not lease or sell their allotted land without federal approval. Afterward, they would be declared "competent," or fit to hold the land on their own. They would be granted citizenship and become subject to all federal and state civil and criminal laws. They would also have the right to sell or lease their land.

The trust period delayed non-Native Americans from being able to buy or lease reservation land. Many wanted to speed up the process. The Burke Act of 1906 was their answer. This act of Congress allowed the Secretary of the Interior to put an early end to the trust period. This could happen by declaring that a Native American was competent ahead of schedule. The effect was to hurry the process by which allotted land was sold or leased to non-Native Americans.

Bursum bill

Legislation to take and use Native American land. The 1922 Bursum bill was one of the earliest attempts to reduce Native American land holdings. The bill was defeated. New Mexico senator Holm O. Bursum introduced the bill on behalf of Albert Fall. Fall was the Secretary of the Interior. He owned land that bordered on Pueblo reservations. Fall wanted to use the reservation land and water. The Fall Indian Omnibus Bill would have given non-Native Americans rights to Pueblo land and water. These rights would have been given on the basis of land claims made before New Mexico achieved statehood. The law might have passed, but John Collier, the future commissioner of Indian Affairs, alerted the Pueblo. They formed the All-Pueblo Council. They also joined with a group in New Mexico and California to oppose the bill. Bursum was defeated, and Fall was forced to resign from the cabinet due to ***conflict of interest***. The group's success encouraged Native Americans and helped Native American policy reform. In 1924, the Pueblo Lands Act established clear ***title*** to Pueblo lands.

Citizenship Act

Federal law. In the case of *McKay* v. *Campbell* (1870), the **Supreme Court** (see p. 85) ruled that Native Americans born as citizens of a Native American nation were not also U.S. citizens. Therefore, most Native Americans lacked the rights granted to citizens under the Constitution. The General Allotment Act (see **allotment policy**, p. 19) gave Native Americans a way to become citizens. It declared they were "fit" to be individual landowners. By the early 1920s, about two out of three Native Americans had become citizens. Many of them served as soldiers in World War I. Their service increased the pressure to give citizenship to all Native Americans. It was also thought that citizenship would speed assimilation of Native Americans. In 1924, Congress passed the Citizenship Act. The act granted citizenship to all Native Americans. Even so, all Native Americans did not immediately have voting rights. Many states restricted their right to vote. The restrictions in Arizona, Maine, and New Mexico were not lifted until after World War II.

Code Talkers

Wartime Navajo communications unit. During World War II, the need to find a code that the enemy could not break became very important. Choctaw speakers had been used in World War I to send messages in the field. Constant repetition eventually made their code easy to break. It was not useful for high-level communication. A similar system was initially used in World War II. In 1942, the Marines realized the Navajo language was harder to understand. At

Medicine for a Code Talker

During World War II, the Navajo Code Talkers used their native language to keep military secrets from the enemy. It was not the only point of contact between their traditional Navajo customs and the non-Native American world. Here one Code Talker recalls how he got malaria on Guadalcanal, an island in the South Pacific—and how his father helped him get better.

Now I did have a hell of a time with malaria: I got it on Guadalcanal. Out of about 6,000 Marines over there, I was among the last 16 to get it. Some of the colonels and generals asked, "How is it with you Navahos? Are you so tough that you don't need to take quinine?" I always said, "I don't know. I had a tough life when I was a little boy."

I came back to San Francisco, where they sent me to a rehabilitation center, and then to a hospital, then home for a month's leave. I was skin and bones. I came back to Gallup where my father met me. He said, "Son, I'm glad you came back alive. . . . I want you to come home with me. I have something for you there." Well, they had a medicine man there for me. They had a sing over me.

Source: Peter Nabokov, *Native American Testimony*

first, nine Navajo were recruited. A code was created based on their language. Military terms were given Navajo terminology—for example, "whale" was used for "battleship" and "chicken hawk" was used for "dive bomber"—and messages were sent in the Navajo language. Soon more than 400 Navajo were recruited to become radio operators in the Pacific. The Navajo code was the only code that wasn't broken during the war. It has been noted that during the first 48 hours of the battle at Iwo Jima, the Code Talkers sent and received more than 800 messages without error. Without them, the Marines would never have taken the island.

Curtis Act

Federal legislation. In 1887, the General Allotment Act (see **allotment policy**, p. 19) allowed Native American lands to be given to individual Native Americans. The Cherokee and Choctaw of **Indian Territory** (see Vol. 1, p. 106) protested in court against allotment of their lands. In 1898, Congress settled the matter with the Curtis Act. The act did away with Native American governments and courts in the Indian Territory. It allowed allotment to proceed there. It ended the self-rule of the **Five Civilized Tribes** (see Vol. 1, p. 103). The act also sped the changeover of Indian Territory. The land had originally been a reserved homeland for Native Americans. By 1907, it was named **Oklahoma** (see p. 81) and admitted to the Union as a state.

Eastman, Charles Alexander

Charles Eastman
(Dover Publications)

Sioux physician. Eastman (1858-1939) received his medical degree from Boston University in 1890. He then joined the **Bureau of Indian Affairs** (BIA) (see Vol. 1, p. 104). He worked as a doctor on Indian reservations until 1903. Eastman later spoke out to end the BIA. He worked at the Pine Ridge Agency in South Dakota and was the only physician to treat victims of the massacre at **Wounded Knee** (see p. 54). Eastman began working for the YMCA in 1895 and established 32 Native American YMCA groups. In 1910, he assisted in the formation of the Boy Scouts of America and the Camp Fire Girls. After **World War I** (see p. 87), he served as president of the **Society of American Indians** (see p. 84). During the 1920s, he was an inspector of reservations. Eastman's many books include *Indian Heroes and Great Chieftains* (1918).

White and Native American members of Friends of the Indian attend an annual meeting in the early 20th century. (Library of Congress)

Friends of the Indian

Group supporting Native American assimilation. In the late 19th century, many reformers believed the solution to the plight of Native Americans was assimilation, or blending Indians into American life. In 1881, novelist **Helen Hunt Jackson** (see p. 35) published *A Century of Dishonor*. This book had a great effect on Native American rights, much like the novel *Uncle Tom's Cabin* by Harriet Beecher Stowe had helped turn many people against slavery in the 1850s. In 1883, Albert Smiley held a series of conferences at Lake Mohonk, near New Paltz, New York. Smiley was a Quaker and a member of the Board of Indian Commissioners. His conferences attracted reformers who called themselves the Friends of the Indian. The movement's leaders included Herbert Welsh, leader of the Indian Rights Association, and Massachusetts senator Henry Dawes, chairman of the Senate Indian Affairs Committee. As a result of the conferences, federal policy toward Native Americans changed. The government wanted to move Native Americans away from reservations and toward assimilation into American society. As a result, special **boarding schools** (see p. 68) were established. These schools were started to reeducate Native American children. Children were required to speak English, wear white people's clothing, and give up their cultures and traditions. By 1900, there were

24 Native American schools that were located away from the reservations. Most were modeled on the Indian School at Carlisle, Pennsylvania. Also to encourage assimilation, the General Allotment Act (see **allotment policy**, p. 19) was passed in 1887. Under this law reservations were to be divided into 160-acre lots and given to Native American families. The Friends of the Indian continued to meet at Lake Mohonk from 1883 to 1916.

Great Depression

International economic collapse, lasting from 1929 to 1941. The Great Depression of the 1930s was a time of increased hardship for almost all Americans, including Native Americans. Native Americans were already accustomed to hardship. For the most part they carried on the same ways of life that they had before the years of the Great Depression. Children still attended boarding schools, and throughout the period they tried to blend their traditions and their cultures into their schooling. Families still needed medical attention. When improved roads made it easier to get to hospitals and clinics in the 1930s, they tried to use them. Native Americans also went on practicing their religions. It was easier to do after 1934, when the Bureau of Indian Affairs prohibited "interference" with Native American religious life.

Even though life stayed the same in many ways, the period saw some important social reforms for Native Americans. Among them were the government programs known as the "Indian New Deal." These programs promoted the practice of Native American crafts and allowed some self-government. The most important legislation of the **New Deal** (see p. 79) era was the **Indian Reorganization Act** (see p. 76). It ended allotment policy, improved education, and allowed Native Americans more freedom to govern themselves.

At the same time, the federal government took several actions that made life harder for Native Americans. One was the reduction in the size of Navajo grazing allotments for sheep. This was a move meant to restore overused land. Instead it brought about a loss of a livelihood for the Navajo. Navajo elder Descheeny Nez (*duh-SHE-nee nez*) Tracy said, "All was going well, and the people had increased their livestock very rapidly, when along came John Collier...and crushed them before our eyes."

Hayes, Ira Hamilton

Ira Hamilton Hayes (National Archives)

Soldier. Ira Hamilton Hayes was a member of the Pima Nation, born in Sacaton (*SAK-uh-tun*), Arizona. He joined the U.S. Marines in 1942 and became a paratrooper in **World War II** (see p. 88) battles in the Pacific. In 1945, he took part in the Fifth Marine division assault on the island of Iwo Jima (*EE-wo JEE-muh*). Hayes was one of six men who raised the American flag atop Mount Suribachi (*soo-ree-BOTCH-ee*). A famous photograph was taken of Hayes and three of the other soldiers raising the flag (see p. 89). The image became an important symbol of freedom. Later, a monument in Washington, D.C. was built to remember the flag-raising event at Iwo Jima.

Indian Arts and Crafts Board

Federal organization. In 1936, Congress founded the Indian Arts and Crafts Board. This board of five people was charged with promoting Native American economic welfare. Native Americans

Young Native Americans at work in a program operated by the Indian Arts and Crafts Board. (National Archives)

were encouraged to practice their traditional arts and crafts. By doing so, other Native Americans could be trained. Also their products could be sold. The board established museums, shops, and other outlets where the public could learn about and buy Native American craft products. Later, Congress passed the Indian Arts and Crafts Act. This act increased the powers of the board. The board could take legal action against non-Native American competitors whose artwork copied the work of the Native Americans.

Indian Defense League

Organization. In 1926, Tuscarora chief Clinton Rickard and David Hill, a Mohawk, founded the Indian Defense League. The league provided legal representation for Native Americans who could not afford it. It was associated mainly with the Six Iroquois Nations of New York and Canada. In 1928, the League established the right of free travel and trade for Iroquois across the border between the United States and Canada.

Indian Reorganization Act (IRA)

Federal legislation, passed in 1934. This act of Congress brought an end to the allotment era. This was a time when the government gave Native American land to individuals. The Indian Reorganization Act provided that Native American lands would be conserved. It also restored Native American governments and protected their cultures and economic development.

Specifically, the Indian Reorganization Act banned further allotment of reservation land. It extended the trust period on lands that had already been allotted. Some of the Native American owners had not yet received full ownership. It provided for Native American nations to be given new lands and to regain some of the surplus lands that had already been opened to sale. It permitted self-government in which the nations could write constitutions and bylaws. The act provided funds for Native American businesses and loans for economic development and training. It established a preference for hiring Native Americans for the jobs in the **Bureau of Indian Affairs** (see Vol. 1, p. 104).

The IRA did not apply in Alaska or **Oklahoma** (see p. 81). It did not give Native Americans all they wanted. However, the

Indian Reorganization Act

One of the benefits that the Indian Reorganization Act (1934) gave to Native American nations was a limited right to govern themselves. They could adopt their own constitutions and bylaws. However, these documents had to be approved by the Secretary of the Interior. The following spells out the conditions for Native American self-government.

Any tribe, or tribes, residing on the same reservation, shall have the right to organize for its common welfare, and may adopt an appropriate constitution and bylaws, which shall become effective when ratified by a majority vote of the adult members of the tribe, or of the adult Indians residing on such reservation, as the case may be, at a special election authorized by the Secretary of the Interior under such rules and regulations as he may prescribe. Such constitution and bylaws when ratified as aforesaid and approved by the Secretary of the Interior shall be revocable by an election open to the same voters and conducted in the same manner as herein above provided. Amendments to the constitution and bylaws may be ratified and approved by the secretary in the same manner as the original constitution and bylaws.

Source: Library of Congress

rights it granted were very important. Some called it the Indian Magna Carta, after the 13th-century document that established English rights.

Ishi (*EE-she*)

Yahi (*YAH-hi*) Indian. In 1911, a thin, exhausted, and frightened Native American entered the Northern California town of Oroville. Ishi (c. 1862-1916) was a light-skinned man and he wore very little clothing. Other Native Americans could not understand his language. ***Anthropologists*** Thomas Waterman and Alfred Kroeber went to examine and talk to him. By adapting words of the Yana language, Waterman was able to talk with the man. They named him Ishi ("man"). They also learned he was the last of the Yahi. The Yahi Nation was thought to be extinct. It was believed that whites killed them in the 1800s. Ishi was taken to San Francisco. He was given work at the University of California's Anthropological Museum. There, he showed visitors how his people once made spearheads and arrowheads. He also provided valuable information about the Yahi and their way of life. Ishi died of illness in 1916. In the end, he had enjoyed the friendship of the whites whom he had feared all his life.

Johnson-O'Malley Act

Legislation for Native American education, passed in 1934. The Indian Reorganization Act was passed in 1934. Just before its passage, the Senate passed a bill proposed by Senator Thomas P. O'Malley. The Johnson-O'Malley Act provided funds to public schools. The funds met the educational, social, economic, and cultural needs of Native American children from reservations. This allowed students to attend mainstream schools rather than boarding schools or on-reservation day schools. Today the Johnson-O'Malley program (JOM) also funds programs in regular schools. These programs are needed to support state educational standards for Native American children.

Meriam Report

Statement on condition of Native Americans. In the 1920s, businessman John D. Rockefeller funded a study. Nine scholars, led by Lewis Meriam, conducted the study. They represented the Brookings Institute. The purpose of the study was to find out about the educational, housing, and medical conditions of Native Americans. The group's 1928 report was called "The Problem of Indian Administration." It was also known as the Meriam Report. The study found that conditions on all levels were severely below standard. Education and housing at Native American boarding schools were poor. People in all regions were living at poverty levels. Infant mortality and disease rates were much higher than in non-Native American regions. For example, tuberculosis was 17 times higher for some Arizona nations than the national average. The report called for the **Bureau of Indian Affairs** (see Vol. 1, p. 104) to be reformed and for the government to fulfill its treaty promises.

Montezuma, Carlos

Physician, political leader. Born Wassaja (*wass-AH-juh*) in about 1865 in Arizona, Carlos Montezuma was a Yavapai (*YAH-vahp-*

eye) (Mohave-Apache). In 1871, he was captured by the Pima and sold to Carlos Gentil. Gentil was a prospector and photographer who renamed him and brought him east. Montezuma earned a B.S. degree in 1884 from the University of Illinois, Urbana, and an M.D. degree in 1889 from the Chicago Medical College. After a brief period of private practice, he began working for the Bureau of Indian Affairs. However, he soon became frustrated by conditions on the western reservations. He served as physician at the Carlisle Indian School in Pennsylvania. Later, he returned to private practice. In 1903, Montezuma helped to create the Fort McDowell Yavapai Reservation. By 1911, he had reclaimed his birth name of Wassaja and become a member of the **Society of American Indians** (see p. 84). Presidents Theodore Roosevelt and Woodrow Wilson both offered him the position of Commissioner of Indian Affairs. He refused and instead worked to abolish the reservation system and Bureau of Indian Affairs. He also spoke out for citizenship for Native Americans. Montezuma founded the Indian magazine *Wassaja* and wrote three books, including *Let My People Go* (1914).

National Congress of American Indians (NCAI)

Native American rights organization. Native American leaders from 27 states founded the NCAI in 1944. It was an early example of a **pan-Indian** (see p. 114) organization. Its goals were to preserve Native American culture and practices and to fight for Native American rights. The NCAI established the **Indian Claims Commission** (see p. 110) in 1946. This commission promoted the passage of the Indian Self-Determination and Education Act (1975). At the end of the 20th century, it had a membership of 200 Native American nations.

Native American Church

(See **peyote religion**, p. 83.)

New Deal

Government programs for jobs and welfare. In 1932, the United States dealt with the effects of the **Great Depression** (see p. 74). Franklin Roosevelt was elected president. He promised the nation a "New Deal" to overcome the Depression. It was to provide employment and security for all its citizens. Roosevelt set out to

John Collier, who respected the Native American value of community spirit over individual gain, spent much of his life fighting to preserve Native Americans' way of life. From 1933 to 1945, he served as commissioner of Indian Affairs in the administration of President Franklin Roosevelt. (National Archives)

change the monetary system. He also set up federal agencies to regulate private industry and create jobs. Many new actions were introduced. Among them was the Works Projects Administration (WPA). Under this program, Americans were employed to build roads, dams, and buildings.

A part of the WPA was the Civilian Conservation Corps (CCC). It hired young men ages 18-25 to work in a national forest program. The CCC gave John Collier, the newly appointed Commissioner of Indian Affairs, a way to relieve Native American hardships. Collier began the Indian Conservation Work Program. The program had $6 million in federal funds. As part

In 1935, President Franklin Roosevelt created the Works Progress Administration (WPA) to help thousands of poor people during the Great Depression. Among those helped were Native Americans. In this photograph, a Native American teacher named Lena Phoenix is shown at her WPA job teaching young Paiute girls to do traditional beadwork. (National Archives)

of the Indian Conservation Work Program, Native Americans constructed dams and roads and made building repairs on 33 reservations. Some members of the Bureau of Indian Affairs resisted the hiring of Native Americans. Collier replaced any staff who refused to cooperate with the program.

In 1935, the WPA program provided even more jobs on federal projects for Native Americans. These jobs resulted in improvements to buildings and roads in many areas. The New Deal also saw the passage of the **Indian Reorganization Act** (see p. 76) of 1934. This act reversed previous government policy to break up reservations and the tribal system. Native American land holdings were saved. In addition, Native American governments were created and Native Americans were given more rights.

Oklahoma

One-time "Indian Territory." During the 1800s, Native Americans were moved into the area called **Indian Territory** (see Vol. 1, p. 106). It included what are now Kansas, Nebraska, and Oklahoma. Kansas and Nebraska, however, became separate states in 1854. The amount of land in the territory was further decreased after the **Civil War** (see p. 27). By 1876, it comprised an area about 350 miles by 200 miles.

Lone Wolf v. *Hitchcock*

The case of *Lone Wolf* v. *Hitchcock* (1903) concerned a Kiowa man named Lone Wolf. Congress had decided to open Kiowa-Comanche lands in Oklahoma for sale to non-Native Americans. Lone Wolf resisted in court, arguing that Native American consent had not been given for the sale in the manner required by the Treaty of Medicine Lodge (1867). In its decision, the Supreme Court ruled that Congress had the power to abrogate, or set aside, the stipulations, or points agreed upon, in an Indian treaty.

The power exists to abrogate the provisions of an Indian treaty, though presumably such power will be exercised only when circumstances arise which . . .demand, in the interests of the country and the Indians themselves, that it should do so. When, therefore, treaties were entered into between the United States and a tribe of Indians it was never doubted that the power to abrogate existed in Congress, and that in a contingency such power might be availed of from considerations of government policy, particularly if consistent with perfectly good faith towards the Indians.

Source: National Archives.

In 1887, Congress passed the General Allotment Act (see **allotment policy**, p. 119). This act broke up reservations and allotted 160 acres of land for each Native American family. The act also produced large areas of surplus land for non-Native American settlers. In 1890, Congress created Oklahoma Territory. This abolished Indian Territory.

By 1896, the land reserved for Native Americans was half the size it had been in 1876. Most Native Americans lived in eastern Oklahoma. Non-Native American settlers lived in the western part of the Territory.

Tensions grew as some Native Americans resisted allotment. The Crazy Snake Uprising in 1901 was led by Chitto Harjo (*HAR-jo*). Harjo was a Creek. He led an armed resistance against the allotment process. Federal forces ended the uprising. Redbirth Smith resisted allotment through civil disobedience. Smith was arrested and forced to enroll in 1902.

In 1907, Oklahoma became the 46th state. The remaining Native American lands were made "***trust*** areas" rather than reservations. Some land was allotted to families or individuals. Native American Nations owned other lands. A 1936 Act of Congress protected Native American lands in Oklahoma from outside land ***speculators***. As of 2000, Oklahoma was home to 392,000 Native Americans, second in the U.S. only to California, which had 628,000. Many still live on Native American lands. Others earn their livings by agriculture or in industries such as oil, small business, manufacturing, retail, and construction.

peyote religion

Religious movement centered on peyote. For thousands of years Native Americans in the Southwest and Mexico used the peyote cactus in their ceremonies. In the 1800s, knowledge of peyote spread to the Great Plains. Peyote was used in the **Ghost Dance religion** (see p. 34). John Wilson was a Caddo/Delaware/French leader of the Ghost Dance religion movement. The government banned the Ghost Dance religion in the 1890s. After the ban, John Wilson began speaking about the holiness of peyote. **Quanah** (*KWAH-nuh*) **Parker** (see p. 42), a Comanche war chief, discovered peyote. After using it, he gave up violence and spent the rest of his life teaching the peyote religion. Many Great Plains Nations were soon following what came to be called the "Peyote Road."

During the 1890s, James Mooney, a Smithsonian ***archeologist***, took part in intertribal religious ceremonies using peyote. He realized its use could unite Native Americans. In 1918, he started the Native American Church, based on the peyote religion. By the 1930s, about half of the U.S. Native American population belonged to the church. Although many attempts were made to end the religion and outlaw peyote use, the church gained strength.

In 1993 and 1994, the Native American Free Exercise of Religion Act overturned an earlier Supreme Court ruling that had made peyote illegal. The act protected the Native American Church and the right for Native Americans to use peyote. Today the church membership is over 250,000. Peyote use for non-Native Americans is still illegal.

Pratt, Richard Henry

U.S. military leader and educator. Born in Rushford, New York, in 1840, Pratt served in the Union army during the **Civil War** (see p. 27). After the war, he was made commander of Indian scouts at Fort Sill. He was in charge of hunting down Native American warriors who had been active in the **Red River War** (see p. 44). Once found, they were taken by Commander Pratt to the Fort Marion Military Prison in St. Augustine, Florida. At the prison, Pratt began a school and job-training center. In 1878, the government released the Native Americans. Pratt accompanied some of them to a training school in Virginia. He became one of the school's teachers.

In 1879, the U.S. War Department asked Pratt to start a school for Native Americans in Carlisle, Pennsylvania. Opened in 1880, the Carlisle Indian School became a model for other **boarding schools** (see p. 68) for Native Americans. Over time, Pratt came to disagree with the U.S. government policy of setting up schools near reservations. He also criticized missionary schools that sent students back into reservations. Because of his criticism of U.S. policy toward Native Americans, he was asked to leave the Carlisle school.

Snyder Act

Congressional ***legislation*** to assist Native Americans. The goal of the **Bureau of Indian Affairs** (see Vol. 1, p. 104) was to oversee all matters concerning Native Americans. However, nothing specific had been provided for the health and welfare of Native Americans. This changed with the passing of the Snyder Act. Under this law it was directed that "the Bureau of Indian Affairs, under the supervision of the Secretary of the Interior, shall direct, supervise, and expand such moneys as Congress may from time to time appropriate, for the benefit, care, and assistance of the Indians throughout the United States." The act included health care, industrial and agricultural assistance, employment, alcohol and drug control, and "general support and civilization, including education." The law, passed in 1921, helped most with health care. By 1926, physicians in the Public Health Service were being sent to the Indian Health Program. The Indian Health Care Act of 1976 built upon the Snyder Act. It further improved the care and education of Native Americans.

Society of American Indians

Native American organization. The Society of American Indians was founded in 1911. It was one of the most powerful Native American rights groups of the early 20th century. The group helped bring about the granting of U.S. citizenship (see **Citizenship Act**, p. 70) for Native Americans. It worked for the assimilation of Native Americans and the end of the **Bureau of Indian Affairs** (see Vol. 1, p. 104). This intertribal group was among the first of its kind. It led the way for future intertribal organizations such as the Indian Defense Association of America (1915). This was a legal group that protected Native American rights.

Supreme Court decisions

Rulings of the nation's highest court. Several Supreme Court decisions from 1891 to 1945 affected Native Americans. Some had a negative effect and some had a positive effect. One positive case was *Talton* v. *Mayes* (1896). In this case, the court ruled that the Cherokee could make laws and punish offenders within their own nation and territory. This was an important step toward upholding Native American self-rule. Native Americans won another victory with *Winters* v. *United States* (1908). In this case, the Supreme Court ruled that Native Americans had the right to have enough water for agricultural uses on their reservations. Known as the **Winters Doctrine** (see p. 87), this decision was important in allowing Native Americans to keep and develop their lands.

Lone Wolf v. *Hitchcock* (1903) hurt Native Americans. In this case, the Supreme Court ruled that Congress had the power to cancel a treaty that was made with Native Americans. This allowed the faster sale of Native American lands to non-Native Americans. Native Americans were often tricked into selling land.

The *U.S.* v. *Sandoval* (1913) case weakened Native American self-rule. It allowed Congress to supervise any communities that were "distinctly Indian." This meant that Native Americans in those communities became "***wards*** of the United States." However, other decisions pointed to the moral responsibility of the United States to treat its wards fairly. The following two decisions, *U.S.* v. *Creek Nation* (1935) and *Seminole Nation* v. *the United States* (1942) are examples. In these cases, the court stressed the responsibility of the United States to exercise care in handling Native American property, such as land and trust fund monies. In *U.S.* v. *Shoshoni* (1938), the court ruled that the United States had to pay the Native American nations when taking timber or minerals from their lands. And in *U.S.* v. *Santa Fe Pacific Railroad Company* (1941), the court restored more than 500,000 acres of land to the Hualapai (*HWAH-lah-pye*) of Arizona.

Thorpe, Jim

Athlete. Native Americans in the early 20th century had few opportunities on the reservation. Some were able to involve themselves in competitive sports. None was better known than James

Jim Thorpe (Library of Congress)

Francis (Jim) Thorpe of the Sac and Fox Nations. Many sports writers considered him the best athlete of the first half of the 20th century. Thorpe first won fame in the 1912 Olympics. He won gold medals in the ***decathlon*** and ***pentathlon***. In the 1920s, he was also a well-known major league baseball and football player.

Other Native American Olympic athletes include Hopi runner Louis Tewanima (*tee-wah-NEE-muh*). He won three medals in the 1912 Olympics. Penobscot runner Andrew Sockalexis (*sock-uh-LEX-is*) also competed in the 1912 games and won second place in that year's Boston Marathon. Onondaga (*on-un-DAHG-uh*) runner Tom Longboat won the 1907 Boston Marathon. Football player John Levi became one of the first Native Americans named to the All-American football team.

Winters Doctrine

The federal reservation of water rights. In the early 1900s, Gros Ventre (*grow vant*) and Assiniboine (*ahs-in-ee-BOYN*) Native Americans lived on the Fort Belknap Reservation in Montana. Their ability to ***irrigate*** their lands was being affected by white settlers' use of the nearby Milk River. The U.S. government brought suit on their behalf. In the case of *Henry Winters* v. *United States of America* (1908), the **Supreme Court** (see p. 85) decided that the Native Americans had reserved rights to the river's water. These rights were based on the 1888 treaty that had created the reservation. The treaty gave priority to the Native Americans' claim. The decision resulted in what has become known as the Winters Doctrine. Using the ruling of the Winters Doctrine, Native Americans have claimed rights to water on or touching land specifically reserved for them. The doctrine has also been applied to national parks and forests, wildlife refuges, and other public areas. These are all areas which the federal government has put aside for a specific purpose. No state can change or ***regulate*** Native American reserved water rights today without special legislation or agreement.

World War I

International military conflict, lasting from 1914 to 1918. Many Native Americans willingly participated in World War I. Their participation in the war against Germany and its allies was promoted by U.S. government leaders. The government believed it would help assimilate Native Americans into mainstream society. Some Native American nations, such as the Oneida (*oh-NYE-duh*) and Onondagas, declared war on Germany themselves. Enlistment numbers for Native Americans totaled 16,000. This rate was twice as high as for other groups during the war.

In combat, some Native Americans were used as scouts. Their commanders drew upon their recent service as trackers against Pancho Villa, a Mexican leader who had raided American towns in the Southwest. General John Pershing organized a team of Apache scouts. Other Native Americans had various jobs. They served in both ***integrated*** and nearly all-Native American units, such as Company E of the 142nd Infantry Regiment. Some members of this unit became **Code Talkers** (see p. 71). Code talking was the use of Native American languages in sending radio messages.

Notable soldiers included Cherokee Sergeant Alfred Bailey, Choctaw Corporal Nicholas E. Brown, and Choctaw Private Joseph Oklahombi (*OK-luh-HOME-bee*). Brown and Oklahombi received France's highest honor, the Croix de Guerre (*CRO-wah de GAYRE*), or Cross of War.

During the war, some Native American farmers in the Plains were persuaded to lease their land to large-scale wheat growers. This helped to fill the increased wartime need for foodstuffs. Leasing their land gave them enough money until wheat prices dropped. Ultimately, a lack of money and lack of ability to modernize left them unable to reclaim their lands.

Some Native Americans refused to register for the draft. They felt that the government had treated Native Americans unjustly. This was their reason for not wanting to serve in a U.S.-led action. Others felt the war served only the rich. Some of these people were involved in the Green Corn Rebellion in **Oklahoma** (see p. 81), a violent battle between a group of 300 white, African American and Native American farmers and Oklahoma National Guard and U.S. Army troops.

During the war, one of the symbols of assimilation ended, when the Carlisle Indian School closed down. It was later used to provide medical facilities for returning war veterans.

Partly in response to their military service in the war, the U.S. government granted citizenship to all Native Americans in 1924.

World War II

International war between 1939 and 1945. More Native Americans participated in World War II than in World War I. More than 25,000 Native Americans served during the war. This number represented one-third of all able-bodied Native American males. In large part, they and the many other Native Americans were greatly changed by the wartime experience. For an extended period, they were part of the larger American military or civilian society. Their service later affected their choice of community and employment and their expectations during the postwar era.

Native Americans were stationed throughout Europe and the Pacific. Some of the battles in which they served include the battles of Midway and Iwo Jima and the Normandy invasion. Hundreds of women served in various branches including the

Ira Hayes of the Pima Nation was one of the marines in this famous photograph taken after the capture of Iwo Jima from the Japanese during World War II (National Archives)

Army Nurse Corps, the WACs, and the Navy. Enlisted members of the Plains peoples, such as the Blackfeet, Comanche, and Kiowa, were particularly courageous. Some 420 Navajo members of the Marines were famous as **Code Talkers** (see p. 71). They used the Navajo language as the basis for military code. There were also seventeen Comanche Code Talkers.

Many individual Native American soldiers received special honors. They included Navajo Robert Nez and Navajo Cozy Stanley Brown, a Code Talker. Congressional Medal of Honor winners include First Lieutenant Jack Montgomery (Cherokee), First Sergeant Ernest Childers (Creek), and Van Barfoot (Choctaw). But none received as much public attention as Pima marine **Ira Hayes** (see p. 75). He was one of the six soldiers who raised an American flag on Mt. Suribachi, Iwo Jima. A photograph of the flag raising was taken and Hayes became nationally known.

On the home front, Native American experiences during World War II were varied. Many Native Americans worked in weapons factories in cities located away from their reservations. Others were responsible for the sale of tens of thousands of *war*

bonds. While the work provided them with new experiences, there was prejudice on many levels. Their housing was often below the standards for other workers. The work was low-level, city life seemed strange, and schedules were rigid.

Some Native American lands were taken for various military uses, including a gunnery range and Japanese-American internment camps. After the Japanese invaded the Aleutian Islands, some Aleuts were brought to live in Alaska. Some Native Americans refused draft registration because of past U.S. mistreatment of Native Americans. Some of the resisters were jailed for up to several years.

CHAPTER THREE

Renewal

Native Americans Today, 1946–Present

"Indians did not discover they were Indians in the early 1970s. We were not reborn; we were simply noticed."

–P. Sam Deloria, Standing Rock Sioux

The period from the end of **World War II** (see p. 88) to the start of the 21st century was one of great change for Native Americans. Their populations grew. Their spirits were revived through new kinds of political activism and a sense of community. Also important were shifting government policies. These included a policy that promoted Native American **self-determination** (see p. 118). This term refers to their right to decide their own affairs.

According to the U.S. Census Bureau, the population of Native Americans and Alaska Natives has grown almost sevenfold since World War II. In 1950, the reported population was 343,410. In 2000, it was 2,475,956. This was a faster rate of growth than the U.S. population as a whole. The U.S. Census Bureau estimates that the Native American population will continue to grow in the future, though at a slower rate. The number of Native Americans is expected to nearly double by the year 2050, to 4.4 million.

For Native Americans, the postwar period began with the establishment of the **Indian Claims Commission** (see p. 110) in 1946. This commission was founded at the urging of the **National Congress of American Indians** (see p. 79). It gave Native American nations a chance to sue for payments for land they had lost. It also led to a growing desire to end the country's obligations toward Native Americans. The federal responsibility for Native Americans was called a *trust* responsibility. This responsibility was seen as a relic of a bygone time, one that looked down on Native Americans and one that cost too much money.

In 1949, the Hoover Commission on the Reorganization of Government recommended a **termination policy** (see p. 119). Termination referred to an end to the federal trust responsibility for Native Americans. Officials who supported termination policy included Dillon Myer and Glenn Emmons. They both served as commissioners of Indian affairs in the 1950s. Supporters of termination wanted to end federal aid to Native American communities. This would be done as soon as the communities were considered to be ready to manage on their own. Termination supporters also wanted to end trust status for reservations. This would make reservations subject to state laws. In a renewed drive for assimilation, or becoming more like the majority of Americans, the termination supporters encouraged Native Americans to relocate to cities.

In the 1950s, the federal government took several actions that made termination the country's official Native American policy. In 1952, a voluntary **relocation** (see p. 116) program was begun to help Native Americans who wanted to move off their reservations to cities. In 1953, Public Law 280 gave certain states criminal and civil control over Native American lands. Many Indian schools were closed and students were shifted to public schools. Care of Native American **health** (see p. 110) was transferred from the Bureau of Indian Affairs to the Public Health Service.

Timeline

1946

The **Indian Claims Commission** is founded to give tribes a way to get payment for lands they have lost.

1949

The Hoover Commission on the Reorganization of Government recommends **termination policy**. This policy ends the federal trust responsibility for Native Americans.

The strongest federal action that supported termination policy was the Termination Resolution, passed by Congress in 1953. This law officially declared that termination was a goal for all Native Americans. It stated that federal trust status should be ended in certain states and for certain nations. From 1954 to 1962, the federal government ended its trust relationship with dozens of nations and other Native American communities.

Many Native Americans opposed termination. The Menominee of Wisconsin suffered economic disaster when their trust status was terminated. Before termination, they were self-sufficient, living off their timber business. Termination brought taxes and loss of federal social services. The result was financial ruin and widespread hardship. The Menominee finally persuaded Congress to restore their trust status in 1974. Most of the other terminated Native American communities also suffered from the policy and eventually had their trust status restored.

The movement for relocation to cities was also costly for many Native Americans. The government gave Native Americans some initial aid to settle in the cities. But without the necessary job training or urban survival skills, many relocated Native Americans became homeless and penniless.

The experience of leaving the reservation for the cities did not help some Native Americans become used to white society. Instead it helped them to become more aware of the bonds they shared with other Native Americans. They formed city-based Native American organizations. The

1952	1953	1953	1961–1963
The federal government starts a voluntary **relocation** program to help Native Americans move from the reservation to cities.	Public Law 280 gives the states of California, Minnesota, Nebraska, Oregon, and Wisconsin criminal and civil control over Native American lands.	Congress passes the Termination Resolution. It allows termination, or the end of federal government assistance, to begin for certain Native American nations and states.	President John F. Kennedy shifts federal Native American policy away from **termination policy**. Under his administration, federal aid to Native Americans increases.

organizations contributed to the growing movement of **pan-Indianism** (see p. 114). "Pan-Indianism" meant emphasizing unity among all Native Americans. Some Native Americans who grew up in the cities and attended college went on to become Native American activists in the 1960s.

By the early 1960s, thoughts were moving away from termination policy. The administration of President John F. Kennedy (1961–1963) decided not to continue it. Native Americans were tired of having their fates controlled by the changing policies of the federal government. By the early 1960s, they were calling for **self-determination** (see p. 118) and **tribal sovereignty** (see p. 123). These terms referred to the right to choose for themselves how to organize their societies and decide what would become of them.

Several commissions in the 1960s condemned the failures of government policy. They supported the need to involve Native Americans in future decisions concerning them. Older Native American organizations, such as the National Congress of American Indians, and new ones such as the **National Indian Youth Council (NIYC)** (see p. 113), founded in 1961, kept pressure on the government to make self-determination into federal policy. The groups also wanted to continue the services and keep the special status they saw as essential to Native American survival.

In part, the government responded to this call. New social programs gave Native Americans more control over federal aid. In 1966, Robert L. Bennett, an Oneida, became the first Native American to hold the office of

1961	1961	1964	1966
The **National Indian Youth Council** is founded.	Several commissions, including the Brophy Commission on the Rights, Liberties, and Responsibilities of the American Indian, support the idea of Native American **self-determination**, or the freedom to govern themselves.	The Economic Opportunity Act allows Native American councils to establish their own community action agencies to run anti-poverty programs.	Robert L. Bennett, an Oneida, becomes the first Native American to hold the office of commissioner of Indian Affairs (see **Bureau of Indian Affairs**, Vol. 1, p. 104) since the 19th century.

commissioner of Indian Affairs since **Ely S. Parker** (see p. 41) in the 19th century. In 1968, President Lyndon B. Johnson proposed "self-determination" as a "new goal for our Indian programs. . . a goal that erases old attitudes of paternalism and promotes partnership self-help." In 1970, President Richard Nixon urged Congress to adopt a Native American policy of self-determination without termination. This meant that Native Americans would have more ability to govern their own affairs, but would also received some financial support from the federal government.

Some Native Americans were impatient with the pace of change. They turned to activism. They organized a variety of protests and demonstrations. The African American civil rights movement and the student movement against the Vietnam War offered models for Native American resistance. Some of the protests became violent. Some African Americans were turning to militant, or aggressive, action with the black power movement. A number of Native Americans began a **red power** (see p. 116) movement. The best known militant Indian group was the **American Indian Movement (AIM)** (p. 99) established in 1968.

In 1969, AIM took part in seizing Alcatraz Island, California. This was the site of a former prison. They took this action to bring attention to all the land that non-Native Americans had seized from Native Americans. The activists stayed at Alcatraz until 1971. In 1972, AIM activists took part in a march on Washington, D.C., called the **Trail of Broken Treaties** (see p. 122).

1968	1968	1969–1971	1970
The **American Indian Movement (AIM)** is founded to protect Native American rights.	Writer **N. Scott Momaday**, a Kiowa, publishes his first novel, *House Made of Dawn.* The novel wins the Pulitzer Prize.	**The American Indian Movement (AIM)** takes part in occupying Alcatraz Island, California.	President Richard Nixon urges Congress to adopt a Native American policy of **self-determination** without an end to government support.

The march ended with a brief occupation of the **Bureau of Indian Affairs** (see Vol. 1, p. 104) offices. In 1973, AIM occupied **Wounded Knee** (see p. 124) on the Pine Ridge Reservation of South Dakota. It was the site of the U.S. massacre of a Sioux group that had ended the Indian Wars in 1890. A 71-day ***siege*** developed. During the siege, two Native Americans were killed and a federal marshal was wounded.

Congress took some steps to meet Native American demands for self-determination without termination. In 1975, Congress passed the Indian Self-Determination and Educational Assistance Act (see **education**, p. 107). This act gave Native American nations more control over federal social programs on their reservations. In 1978, the American Indian Freedom of Religion Act protected Native American rights to practice their religions. The Indian Child Welfare Act and the Tribally Controlled Community College Assistance Act extended control by Native American nations over child custody and education issues.

Native Americans took new kinds of action to increase their powers over their own affairs. The experience of political activism gave many of them a new pride in their heritage. They were ready for political involvement. **The Native American Rights Fund (NARF)** (see p. 113) was founded in 1970. It provided legal representation for Native American Nations. NARF has assisted nations in hundreds of legal cases on many issues. These cases include land claims, water rights, hunting and fishing rights, and federal recognition of their status as

1970	1972	1973	1975
The Native American Rights Fund (NARF) is founded to provide legal representation for Native American nations.	AIM participates in a march on Washington, D.C., called the **Trail of Broken Treaties**. The march ends with an occupation of the Bureau of Indian Affairs building.	AIM members occupy **Wounded Knee** on the Pine Ridge Reservation of South Dakota. A siege there lasts for 71 days.	At the Pine Ridge Reservation, two FBI agents are killed. **Leonard Peltier**, a Sioux, is found guilty. He is given two life sentences. Many Native Americans and others believe he is innocent.

nations. Some of the most important cases have involved the right of nations to govern themselves. The **Supreme Court decision** (see p. 85) in *Santa Clara* v. *Martinez* (1978) was a victory in that struggle.

Conditions for Native Americans—in health, education, and employment—had improved by the end of the 1970s. However, in the 1980s, President Ronald Reagan cut government spending on social programs. Unemployment rose to as high as 95 percent for some nations. By the end of the decade, gambling became a new source of income for some nations. The Supreme Court and Congress agreed that Native Americans had the right to run gaming operations, including casinos (see **gaming and casinos**, p. 108), on their reservations. Gaming was allowed even if it was banned elsewhere in the state. Gaming revived the economies of Native American nations, especially in the Northeast.

Issues of self-determination and the federal government's ***trust*** responsibility continue to be concerns for Native Americans. Native Americans have defended the sovereignty of their nations. However, they have opposed the end of federal aid and protection. The current status of Native American nations is similar to that of states. They support and govern themselves to a certain extent. They are also subject to some restrictions in exchange for federal aid.

In some ways, Native Americans since the 1970s have been enjoying an "Indian Renaissance." Their arts are thriving and their traditional cultures are being passed on to the young (see **traditional ways**, p. 120). This happens through gatherings known as **powwows** (see p. 115), which celebrate Native American

1975	1977	1985	1987
The Council of Energy Resource Tribes (CERT) is founded to protect Native American nations' mineral resources.	The **American Indian Policy Review Commission**, established by Congress in 1972, releases a report recommending that the Bureau of Indian Affairs be closed and Native American Nations be granted greater freedom to govern themselves.	The National Indian Gaming Association is established. This begins a trend toward use of **gaming and casinos** as a source of income for Native American nations.	Cherokee leader **Wilma Mankiller** becomes the first woman to head a major Native American nation.

identity. Among the best-known Native Americans today are Senator **Ben Nighthorse Campbell** (see p. 102) of Colorado, nonfiction writer **Vine Deloria, Jr.** (see p. 104), and novelists **N. Scott Momaday** (see p. 112) and **Louise Erdrich** (see p. 108).

Some negative stereotypes about Native Americans continue. However, most non–Native Americans have a positive image of Native Americans. Institutions such as the National Museum of the American Indian, authorized by Congress in 1989, bring Native American culture and history to a wide audience. Greater respect is paid to Native American remains and sacred objects (see **repatriation of remains**, p. 117). The passage of the Native American Graves Protection and Repatriation Act (1990) requires federal agencies and museums to return remains and sacred objects to the Native American nations from which they came.

Native Americans have increased their populations, made economic gains (see **economics**, p. 105), and renewed their cultural heritages. However, they continue to face problems. They are more likely to be poor, sick, unemployed, or poorly educated than the general population. Certain health problems, such as alcoholism and diabetes, are common among them. Native Americans are a small minority—less than 1 percent of the U.S. population, according to the 2000 Census. The majority of Americans easily forget them. Still, Native Americans remain a vital and growing part of the country.

1990	1996	2000	2002
The Native American Graves Protection and Repatriation Act requires federally funded museums and other institutions to return to Native American nations the remains of their dead.	Native Americans file their largest class-action suit ever. The suit claims that the Department of the Interior mismanaged money and land held in trust.	According to the U.S. Census Bureau, the population of Native Americans and Alaska natives is 2,475,956.	John B. Herrington flies aboard the U.S. space shuttle *Endeavor*, becoming the first Native American in space.

A-Z of Key People, Events, and Terms

American Indian Movement (AIM)

Native American activist group. In 1968, 200 Native Americans met in Minneapolis. They discussed education, employment, housing, police brutality, and government policy toward Native Americans. As a result of this conference, the American Indian Movement (AIM) was founded. The leaders of AIM included Clyde Bellecourt, Dennis Banks, and Russell Means. The role of AIM was to protect Native American rights to **self-determination** (see p. 118) and to preserve the sovereignty of Native American nations. The American public first became aware of AIM in 1969. The leaders took part in seizing Alcatraz (*AL-cuh-traz*) Island. The island

Breaking into Alcatraz

From 1969 to 1971, activists from the American Indian Movement (AIM) took part in occupying Alcatraz Island. The small, rocky island in San Francisco Bay, California, was the site of a former federal prison. The activists issued the following proclamation. It mocks the language of U.S. treaties with Native Americans, recalls the purchase of Manhattan Island for $24, and makes fun of the notion of a Caucasian-run "Bureau of Indian Affairs."

We, the Native Americans, reclaim the land known as Alcatraz Island, in the name of all American Indians by right of discovery. We will purchase Alcatraz Island for twenty-four (24) in glass beads and red cloth, a precedent set by the white man's purchase of a similar island about 300 years ago.

We will give to the inhabitants of the island a portion of the land for their own to be held in trust by the American Indian Affairs and by the bureau of Caucasian Affairs to hold in perpetuity [forever]—for as long as the sun shall rise and the rivers go down to the sea. We will further guide the inhabitants in the proper way of living.

Source: Fourth World Documentation Project.

Dennis Banks, right, one of the founders of the American Indian Movement, is seen with an unidentified fellow member of the group during the siege at Wounded Knee. (Photo by Richard Erdoes)

was the site of a former prison in San Francisco Bay. AIM claimed Alcatraz Island as Native American land and stayed there for 19 months. Other takeovers of federal property followed this action. In 1972, AIM organized a march in Washington, D.C. It was known as the **Trail of Broken Treaties** (see p. 122). The march ended with a six-day occupation of the **Bureau of Indian Affairs** (see Vol. 1, p. 104) building. (The Bureau of Indian Affairs had historically been led by non–Native Americans.) In 1973, more than 2,200 Native Americans took over the hamlet of **Wounded Knee**, South Dakota (see p. 124). They were besieged by U.S. armed forces for 71 days.

AIM has been criticized for using radical means to make public their causes. Some of the group's leaders have been imprisoned for their actions. Yet over the years, AIM has also started programs to assist Native Americans. It has also brought about federal, state, and local policy changes through peaceful measures. Its accomplishments include the establishment of health care boards, job-training programs, legal centers, and housing projects; improvements in Native American **education** (see p. 107) and its funding; and the preservation of Native American history and culture.

American Indian Policy Review Commission

Policy review group established by Congress. In January 1972, an act of Congress created the American Indian Policy Review

Native American Writers

Many Native Americans have written about their struggle to keep their sense of tradition and heritage alive, while also finding a place for themselves and their families in the wider world. Below are some of those authors and some of their most famous works. For a list of other Native American books, especially for young people, see "Resources," starting on page 131.

Name	Nation	Major Work
Sherman Alexie	Spokan/ Coeur D'Alene	Stories: *The Toughest Indian in The World* (2000)
Mary Crow Dog	Sioux	Autobiography: *Lakota Woman* (1991)
Vine Deloria, Jr.	Sioux	Nonfiction: *Custer Died for Your Sins* (1969)
Michael Dorris	Modoc	Novel: *Yellow Raft in Blue Water* (1987)
Louise Erdrich	Ojibwa	Novel: *Love Medicine* (1984)
Joy Harjo	Creek	Poetry: *How We Became Human* (2002)
Thomas King	part Cherokee	Novel: *Green Grass, Running Water* (1993)
N. Scott Momaday	Kiowa	Novel: *House Made of Dawn* (1968)
Leslie Marmon Silko	Pueblo	Novel: *Almanac of the Dead* (1991)

Commission. Its members were three senators, three congressmen, and five Native Americans. Of the Native American members, three were from federally recognized nations, one was from a nonrecognized nation, and one was from a city. The commission set up 11 task forces to review federal policy toward Native Americans. In 1977, the commission presented its report to Congress. Of these, the most important was to replace the **Bureau of Indian Affairs** (see Vol. 1, p. 104) with an independent Native American agency. The commission also recommended that Native American governments should be able to negotiate directly for services. Prior to the recommendation, the BIA was providing the services. Congress failed to act on the commission's recommendations. This was due in part to the fears of some western legislators. They believed voter reaction would be against allowing Native Americans to govern themselves. The BIA's role in Native American affairs began to decrease over the following years. In the late 1980s, Congress approved a Tribal Self-

Ben Nighthorse Campbell (Library of Congress)

Governance Demonstration Project. This project further reduced the BIA's authority. It also gave money and the right of **self-determination** (see p. 118) to some nations.

Campbell, Ben Nighthorse

U.S. senator from Colorado. Campbell, born in 1933, was the son of a Northern Cheyenne and a Portuguese immigrant. He served with the Air Force (1951-1953) and was a member of the U.S. Olympic judo team (1964) (see **sports,** p. 119). Campbell combined jewelry making with a political career. He was the second Native American to serve in the Colorado legislature (1983-1986). He was elected to the U.S. Congress in 1987. In 1992, he became the first Native American to be elected to the Senate in over 60 years. He was reelected in 1998. As a senator, Campbell has worked to preserve the wilderness and to protect Native American water rights. In 1991, he won a battle to rename the Custer National Monument as Little Bighorn Battlefield National Monument. He also sponsored bills to create the National Museum of the American Indian at the Smithsonian. As of 2003, he was the only Native American serving in either house of Congress.

civil rights

Movement to recognize and protect Native American rights. Prior to the **Citizenship Act** of 1924 (see p. 70), Native Americans had virtually no legal rights. The Civil Rights Act of 1866, which granted citizenship to all native-born Americans, did not include Native Americans. After the 1924 act, some states still did not allow Native Americans to vote in state or local elections. This was because they lived on reservations under a federal ***trust***. Finally, in 1948, state laws in Arizona that prevented Native Americans from voting were declared illegal. Soon, other states, such as Maine in 1954 and New Mexico in

1962, granted Native Americans voting rights. The **National Congress of American Indians** (see p. 79), formed in 1944, joined in the work of the growing civil rights movement. NCAI promoted Native American culture and **education** (see p. 107). It also helped Native Americans with legal issues. In 1946, NCAI established the **Indian Claims Commission** (see p. 110) to settle land claims.

In 1961, civil rights groups became more ***militant*** in aspect. The **National Indian Youth Council (NIYC)** (see p. 113) was formed. NIYC began to organize public actions to draw attention to Native American concerns. The 1964 Civil Rights Act banned discrimination on the basis of color, race, religion, or national origin. The 1965 Voting Rights Act confirmed equal enfranchisement for all U.S. citizens.

In 1968, the American Indian Civil Rights Act gave the rights found in the Bill of Rights to Native Americans living on reservations. This prevented states from taking legal control over reservations. It also gave Native American governments a relationship similar to that between the federal and state governments. With these advances, young Native Americans saw the need for even stronger action. This led to the formation of the **American Indian Movement (AIM)** (see p. 99) in 1968. Two years later, the **Native American Rights Fund** (see p. 113) was established. It provided legal and financial protection for Native Americans nationally.

As the civil rights movements became stronger, more laws were passed. These laws include the American Indian Religious Freedom Act of 1978 and the Native American Graves Protection and Repatriation Act of 1990 (see **repatriation of remains**, p. 117).

Crow Dog, Leonard

Sioux medicine man and activist; Crow Dog is a medicine man and activist with the **American Indian Movement (AIM)** (see p. 99) and other groups. He was involved in the 71-day siege of **Wounded Knee** (see p. 124), South Dakota. He was captured by the U.S. and put on trial. He was sentenced to 23 years in prison. As a medicine man, he was active in preserving traditional religion (see **traditional ways**, p. 120). His family history is told in the book, *Crow Dog: Four Generations of Sioux Medicine Men*. Crow Dog was married to **Mary Crow Dog** (see p. 104).

Crow Dog, Mary (Mary Brave Bird)

Lakota writer and activist. Born Mary Brave Bird in 1953, she was raised on reservations. She became active in Native American rights movements as a teenager and was present at **Wounded Knee** (see p. 124) in 1973. She met and married medicine man **Leonard Crow Dog** (see p. 103). In 1990, she published *Lakota Woman*. This autobiography traced her life from troubled childhood to activist adulthood. In 1993, she published another autobiographical work, *Ohitika Woman*. In the book, she tells of her involvement with Leonard Crow Dog and her life as an activist, spouse, and mother. Since their divorce, she has returned to using her maiden name.

Deloria, Vine, Jr.

Lawyer, activist. Vine Deloria, Jr., was born in South Dakota in 1933 into a Hunkpapa Lakota (*luh-KOH-tuh*) Sioux family. He served in the Marine Corps (1954–1956), earned his B.A. degree

A Leave-Us-Alone Law

In *Custer Died for Your Sins: An Indian Manifesto* (1969), Vine Deloria, Jr., a Standing Rock Sioux, attacked U.S. Native American policy. He spoke out for the Native Americans' traditional communal way of life, called tribalism. In the following excerpt, he urges non-Native Americans to let Native Americans live in their own way.

Some years ago at a Congressional hearing someone asked Alex Chasing Hawk, a council member of the Cheyenne River Sioux for 30 years, "Just what do you Indians want?" Alex replied, "A leave-us-alone law."

The primary goal and need of Indians today is not for someone to feel sorry for us and claim descent from Pocahontas to make us feel better. Nor do we need to be classified as semi-white and have programs and policies that bleach us further. Nor do we need further studies to see if we are feasible. We need a new policy by Congress acknowledging our right to live in peace. . . .We need the public at large to drop the myths in which it has clothed us for so long. We need fewer and fewer "experts" on Indians. What we need is a cultural leave-us-alone agreement, in spirit and in fact.

Source: Vine Deloria, Jr., *Custer Died for Your Sins*

Vine Deloria, Jr. (Library of Congress)

(1958) and then a B.D. degree in theology (1963). He was executive director of the **National Congress of American Indians (NCAI)** (see p. 79) from 1964 to 1967. Deloria studied for a law degree and graduated from the University of Colorado in 1970. He became a teacher and an activist for Native American rights. Deloria was a witness for the defense in the 1974 trial of Russell Means and Dennis Banks. They were on trial for their roles in the **Wounded Knee** siege (see p. 124). Deloria has also worked for such organizations as the Council on Indian Affairs, the Institute for the Development of Indian Law, and the Indian Rights Association. His first book, *Custer Died for Your Sins* (1969), reexamined Native American history and argued for **self-determination** (see p. 118). He has written many other books about the history, culture, and treatment of Native Americans, including *Behind the Trail of Broken Treaties* (1985), *God Is Red* (1994), and *Tribes, Treaties, and Constitutional Tribulations* (2000). Today he remains one of the strongest speakers for the rights of Native Americans.

economics

Since the end of World War II, the economic advancement of Native Americans has been steady, but uneven. **Education** (see p. 107) levels improved throughout the period. The percentage

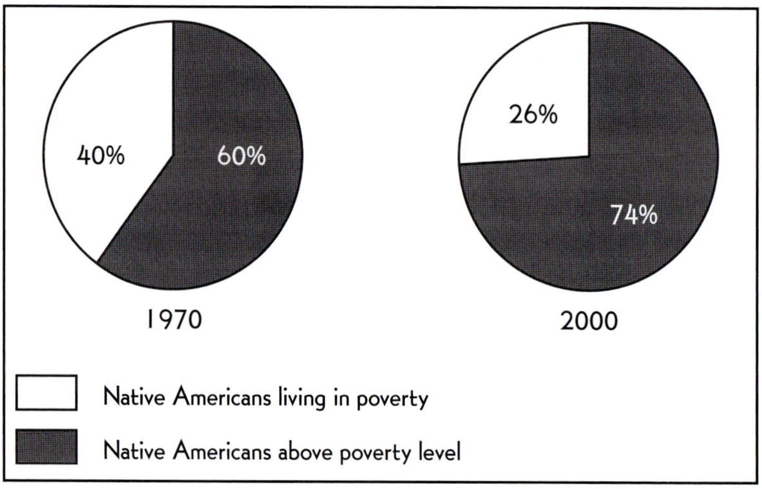

Although the number of Native Americans living in poverty fell from 40 percent to 26 percent between 1970 and 2000, it is still higher than the national average. Source: U.S. Census

of Native American adults 25 years and older who were high school graduates rose to one-third of all students. College attendance among Native Americans doubled. Yet, educational gains did not always mean better economic conditions. In 1970, the Native American median family income was $5,832, versus a national average of $9,590. In addition, about 40 percent of the Native American population lived below the federal poverty level.

To find jobs, many Native Americans moved from reservations. They found work in Native American agencies and in health-related areas. This was possible in part through government programs such as the Indian Self-Determination and Educational Assistance Act, 1975. Native Americans also used their lands to make money. They leased the lands, which were rich in resources, to energy companies. Some Native Americans developed the lands themselves. They were able to create jobs for their people in the process.

Other job areas included tourism. Native Americans built tourist sites at reservations in New Mexico and Arizona. Tourist traffic was high, but not much money reached Native Americans. Most of it went to nonreservation businesses. More successful was tourist **gaming and casinos** (see p. 108). On- and off-reservation gaming was established. Reservation gambling has become as popular. It has provided steady sources of income for some nations.

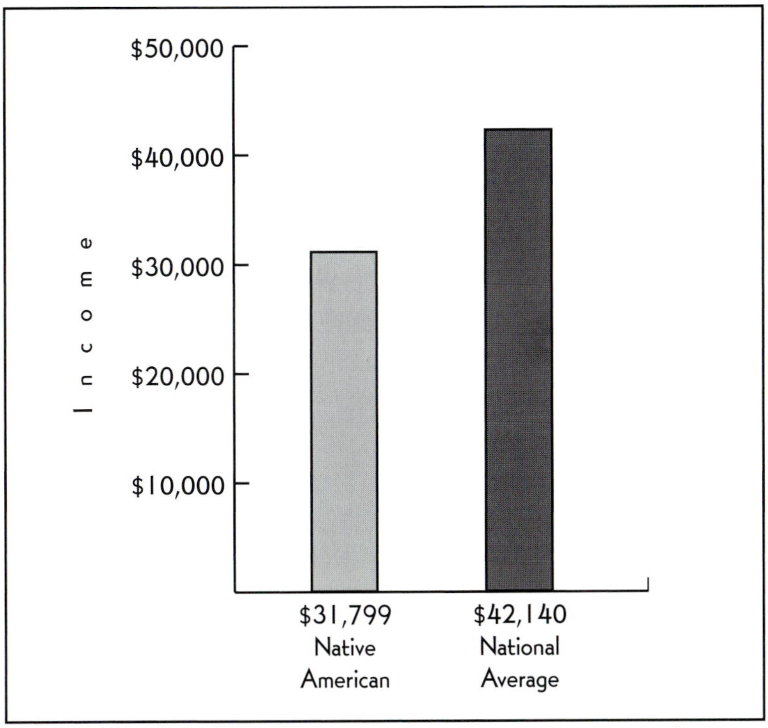

Between 1998 and 2000, the average annual income for Native Americans was $31,799, well under the national average of $42,140 for all Americans. Source: U.S. Census

While great poverty still exists among Native Americans, income levels have risen steadily. The average annual income from Native Americans between 1998 and 2000 was $31,799, still below the national average of $42,140. However, the percentage of Native Americans living below the poverty level fell from 40 percent in 1970 to about 26 percent in 2000.

education

The **Indian Reorganization Act (IRA)** of 1934 (see p. 76) recommended improvements in Native American schooling. However, change was slow in coming. For instance, in 1956 the Bureau of Indian Affairs (BIA) set up an adult training program. Two years later the federal government instituted a **termination policy** (see p. 119). The new policy cut assistance to Native Americans, including many college scholarships and programs.

The late 1960s saw major positive changes. The most important change was the Indian Education Act (IEA) of 1972. It created new educational opportunities for Native American children and their elders and increased the educational standards for Native Americans. It also created an Office of Indian Education and a National Advisory Council for Indian Education (composed of 15 Native Americans and Alaskan natives). The council provided guidance to those responsible for carrying out the act.

The Indian Self-Determination and Education Assistance Act (1975) recognized the need to create public schools on or near reservations. This and other measures taken over the last 30 years have shown that the government better understands Native American education problems and the need to improve them. However, statistics from a 1995 federal government report highlight differences in educational achievement. In that year, only about 9 percent of all Native Americans older than 25 years old had four or more years of college education. That percentage was far below the national average of more than 20 percent.

On January 9, 2002, President George W. Bush signed the No Child Left Behind Act of 2001. It is meant to provide equal education to all students. According to one section of the act, elementary and secondary schools operated by the BIA will also have more financial flexibility to carry out programs.

Erdrich, Louise

Ojibwa novelist and poet. Erdrich was born in Little Falls, Minnesota. She attended Dartmouth College and conducted poetry workshops in North Dakota. Erdrich published the novel *Love Medicine* (1984). The novel, which was about several generations of two Ojibwa families, won the National Book Critics Circle award. Other novels include *The Beet Queen* (1986) and *Tracks* (1988). She was married to Modoc author and scholar Michael Dorris. Together, they wrote *The Crown of Columbus* (1991).

Louise Erdrich
(Photo by Michael Dorris)

gaming and casinos

Games of chance have been common to traditional Native American entertainment. Among the types of games played are guessing games such as the moccasin game, treasure searches, human and horse races, and dice games.

The move toward using gaming as a source of income began in the 20th century. During the mid-century, reservations held bingo games. Gaming was further promoted by a 1976 U.S. **Supreme**

Mohegan Sun in Connecticut is one of the most sucessful Native American–owned casino-resorts in the United States. (Courtesy of Mohegan Sun Resort)

Court decision (see p. 85). This decision ruled that the U.S. government could not regulate activities on Native American lands. In 1985, the National Indian Gaming Association was founded. Its goal was to support those who wanted financial control over gaming on reservations.

During the 1990s, over 150 casinos opened. Some are located on reservation lands. Others are on lands away from reservations. Native Americans purchased much of this nonreservation land. Among successful casinos are Connecticut's Foxwoods Hotel Resort Casino, opened in 1992. Mohegan (*mow-HEE-gun*) Sun Resort, also in Connecticut, opened in 1996. Foxwoods has reported higher earnings than similar casinos in Atlantic City or Las Vegas.

Not every casino is successful. Many that are located in more isolated regions of Great Plains states are less successful than those in busy, heavily populated regions such as the Northeast and California. Yet these same Great Plains states are home to a large number of the poorest Native Americans, who could most use the benefits that successful casinos could bring. Critics of Indian casinos have noted that some nations that own successful casinos have very few members, so the benefits of success only reach a few. Some Native Americans, such as the Navajo, argue that modern-day gambling and casinos promote activities that go against traditional values.

health

For Native Americans, overall health improved in the years since World War II, and life spans increased. However, they did not match the health and life expectancy levels of the rest of the U.S. population. According to the Indian Health Service, average life expectancy in 1969 for a Native American male was 64 years. For non-Native Americans in 1969, life expectancy was 70.5 years. By 2002, Native American life expectancy improved to 71.1 years, although it was still below the national average of 75.5.

Poor conditions also have generated health problems for Native Americans. Pollution in areas where Native Americans live also brought various diseases. One of them, mercury poisoning, affected many members of the Ojibwa (*oh-JIB-way*) of Grassy Narrows in northern Ontario. The cause of the disease was traced to pollution of the English/Wabigoon (*wah-bi-GOON*) River. The pollution was brought on by the many tons of mercury that were dumped in the river by the Reed Paper Company in 1970. In 1993, Navajo and other southwestern peoples were stricken with hantavirus (*HAN-tuh-vy-rus*). Over a dozen deaths were attributed to the viral disease carried by rodents.

Poverty and the fact that some reservations are very isolated may contribute to high suicide rates among Native Americans, say some experts. In one Wyoming Native American community, Wind River, the suicide rate in 1985 was nearly 20 times higher than the national average. In 1988, the suicide rate among Native Americans was twice as high as it was for all Americans. Although programs have been put in place to help prevent suicide among Native Americans, by 2001, the national suicide rate for Native Americans was still 70 percent higher than the rate for Americans in general.

Indian Claims Commission

Committee to settle land claims. In 1946, efforts by the **National Congress of American Indians (NCAI)** (see p. 79) led to the formation of the Indian Claims Commission. Previously, Indian land claims could take 15 years or more to process. The Indian Claims Commission Act gave Native Americans payments for the loss of lands taken by fraud or broken treaties. The commission has handled over 850 claims. More than $800 million has been awarded on 60 percent of the cases it heard. However, awards were made based on the value of the land at the time it was taken. Claimants were not allowed to recover the land itself. Some, including the Hopi (*HO-pee*) and Sioux, refused to cash the checks they received. Others pursued a different legal route. In rare cases, some have succeeded in taking back their land. The Taos Pueblo regained 48,000 acres in 1970, and in 1972 the Yakima (*YAK-ee-muh*) received back 21,000 acres. In 1978, the work of the Indian Claims Commission ended. Remaining cases were transferred to the U.S. Court of Claims. Since then, Native Americans have continued to win payments for loss of land. In 1980, for example, the Penobscot and Passamoquoddy nations settled a suit against Maine and the federal government. The two nations were awarded $81 million.

Not all Native Americans agree with the idea of accepting money for lost lands. For example, in 1987, Senator Bill Bradley introduced a bill to turn most of the Black Hills National Forest in South Dakota over to the Sioux Nation. In addition, the Sioux would have been paid for the use of the lands by the United States

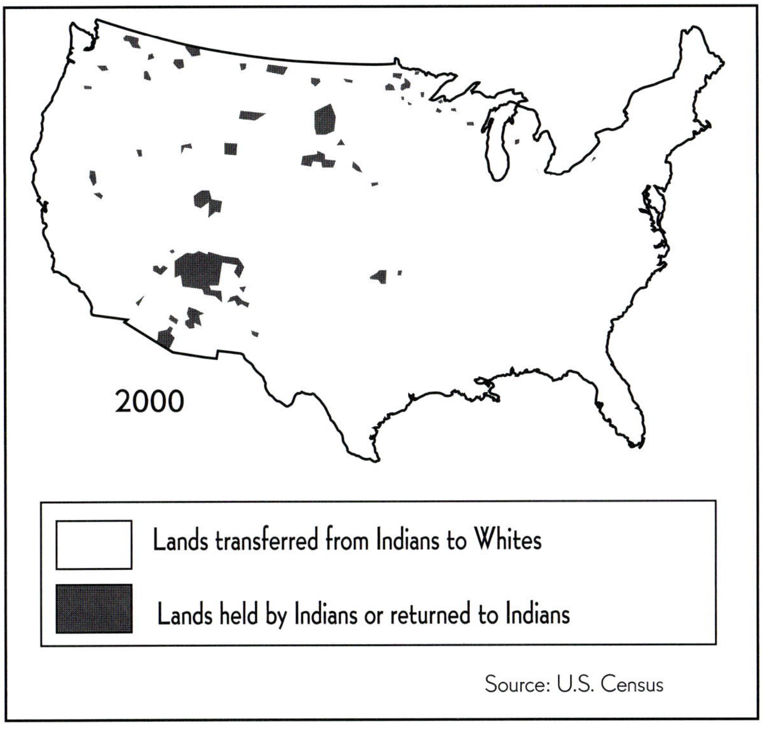

Wilma Mankiller (Courtesy of Wilma Mankiller)

since 1877. Although many Sioux have argued in favor of accepting the money and land, not all have. Some have argued that far more land should be turned over than the 1.2 million acres proposed. Others have said that there was no way to put a financial value of the land, since its value is holy to the Sioux. As of 2002, the land's value had reached $400 million dollars, but none of the money had yet been accepted by the Sioux.

Mankiller, Wilma Pearl

Cherokee leader, activist. Wilma Mankiller was born in 1945 in Oklahoma. She was raised on Mankiller Flats, her family's farm. She was a social worker during the 1960s. In the mid-1970s, Mankiller obtained a college degree in social science and started projects to improve Cherokee communities. Mankiller was elected deputy principal chief of the Cherokee in 1985. She was elected principal chief in 1987 and again in 1991. She was the first woman to head a major Native American nation. She left the post in 1995. During her service, Mankiller began the Institute for Cherokee Literacy (see also **women's rights**, p. 124).

Momaday, Navarre Scott

Kiowa-Cherokee poet and novelist. Momaday is known as N. Scott Momaday. He was born in Lawton, Oklahoma, in 1934 and was raised on various reservations in the Southwest. He attended Virginia Military Academy and the University of New Mexico. Momaday taught on an Apache reservation and began to write poetry. He attended Stanford University and earned a Ph.D. (1963). He became a professor at the University of California, Santa Barbara, and the University of California, Berkeley. His 1968 novel, *House Made of Dawn*, won the Pulitzer Prize for fiction. The novel was about difficulties faced by a Pueblo World War II veteran upon his return home. He was the first Native American to win a Pulitzer Prize. He has written two autobiographies—*The Way to Rainy Mountain* (1969) and *The Names* (1976)—as well as another novel, *The Ancient Child* (1989). In his works, his goal is to preserve oral Native American traditions.

N. Scott Momaday
(Library of Congress)

National Indian Youth Council (NIYC)

The National Indian Youth Council (NIYC) is considered to be the first militant Native American group in North America. It was formed in 1961. That year, the American Indian Conference held its first meeting in Chicago with 500 delegates from 67 Native American nations. Most were also closely involved with the **National Congress of American Indians (NCAI)** (see p. 79). The conference called for greater Native American involvement in government programs and decisions affecting Native Americans. Some of the younger delegates wanted more immediate and direct action. Clyde Warrior, a Ponca, and Melvin Thom, a Paiute (*PYE-oot*), joined with others in founding the NIYC. They produced a newspaper called *ABC: Americans Before Columbus*. They also held events to bring attention to the problems of Native Americans. In 1964, the NIYC sponsored "fish-ins" along rivers in Washington State. The "fish-ins" were in support of Native American fishing rights. Today the NIYC operates out of Albuquerque, New Mexico. It provides job and training opportunities.

Native American Rights Fund (NARF)

Nonprofit Native American civil rights organization. The Native American Rights Fund was founded in 1970. Its goal was to represent Native American nations in legal cases. Many of its lawyers have been Native Americans, including John Echohawk (*ECK-oh-hawk*), a Pawnee. Echohawk has been director of NARF since 1973. In its first two decades, NARF gave legal help to more than a hundred Native American nations in more than a thousand cases. Its cases have involved a variety of issues: land claims, water rights, Native American rights guaranteed by treaties, Native American nations' rights to self-rule, protection of Native American nations' natural resources, religious freedom, return of sacred objects and

The Alaska Native Brotherhood was one of the first pan-Indian groups of the 20th century. Members of the group are seen here preparing for a march in the 1940s. (Smithsonian Institution)

human remains, federal recognition of Native American nations, and individual rights. NARF has helped achieve many of the victories that Native Americans have won in these areas in federal courts.

pan-Indianism

Inter-tribal movement. The expression "pan-Indianism" is described as action by Native Americans of many different nations united together in a common cause. The term covers legal and cultural activities, goals, and organizations of all native peoples. An early step in the history of pan-Indianism was the 1911 formation of the **Society of American Indians** (see p. 84). The **Alaska Native Brotherhood** (see p. 63), founded in 1912, and the Indian Defense Association, created in 1915, quickly followed this group. In 1944, Native American employees of the BIA founded the **National Congress of American Indians (NCAI)** (see p. 79). In the 1960s and 1970s, a younger group began protesting in a more active way. The American Indian Chicago conference of 1961 included members from 67 nations. Many of these had close ties to the NCAI. This conference issued a Declaration of Indian Purpose. The declaration called for more involvement in federal programs that affected the lives of Native Americans. In 1968, the **American Indian Movement (AIM)** (see p. 99) was formed. By the 1990s, inter-tribal cooperation came through such organizations as the Council of Energy Resources Tribes (CERT) and the **Native American Rights Fund (NARF)** (see p. 113).

Peltier, Leonard

Native American activist. An Ojibwa and Lakota Sioux, Leonard Peltier was born in 1944 in North Dakota. In the late 1960s, he joined the **American Indian Movement (AIM)** (see p. 99). He took part in the 1972 **Trail of Broken Treaties** (see p. 122) march and the 1973 siege at **Wounded Knee** (see p. 124). In 1975 at the Pine Ridge Reservation, two FBI agents were killed. Peltier was indicted for their murder. He was found guilty and given two life sentences. AIM has claimed the evidence against him and the trial was prejudiced by anti-AIM sentiment. Peltier supporters also claim that his work against nuclear mining in the Black Hills of South Dakota has made him a political prisoner.

Leonard Peltier (Courtesy of AIM)

powwow

A gathering of Native Americans. The term "powwow" comes from a Narragansett word for a shaman, or religious expert. Today, it refers to a social gathering or celebration of Native Americans anywhere in the country. Often, powwows bring together Native Americans from many Nations. They serve as a way to strengthen the ties of **pan-Indianism** (see p. 114). Traditional dances are featured, and sometimes there are competitions. One example of an annual powwow is the American Indian Exposition-Parade in Anadarko, Oklahoma. Native American foods and crafts are available at powwows. This helps keep Native American culture alive. Often, non–Native Americans are invited. Many powwows are held once a year. (See also **traditional ways**, p. 120.)

A traditional dancer performs a hoop dance at a powwow in Arizona. (Arizona Department of Tourism)

red power

Twentieth-century political movement. The red power movement began in the northwestern U.S. It formed to protest a 1960s Supreme Court ruling concerning Native American fishing rights. Shortly after, the **American Indian Movement (AIM)** (see p. 99) was formed. Its goal was to organize for red power and other related causes. Among red power/AIM actions were the seizures of Alcatraz Island in California (1969–1971) and of the village of **Wounded Knee** (see p. 124) in South Dakota (1973).

relocation policy

U.S. government plan for moving Native Americans into cities. In the 1950s, the U.S. government began a program to help move Native Americans into mainstream society by encouraging them to move to cities. Through it, Native Americans would receive aid in finding housing and jobs. In 1952, the Bureau of

Indian in the Big City

In the decades after World War II, many Native Americans moved to urban areas for the first time. The hardest part of moving to the big city was feeling homesick for the land and people they had left behind. In the passage below, Belle Jean Francis, an Athapascan, describes the experience of trying to adjust to Chicago in 1968.

Here I am in the big city, right in the middle of Chicago. I don't know anybody. I am so lonesome and have that urge to go home. I don't know which direction to go—south, north, east, or west. . . . I see strange faces around me and I keep wondering how I will survive in this strange environment. I just keep wondering how I can get over this loneliness, and start adjusting to this environment. I know I have to start somewhere along the line and get involved in social activities and overcome the fear I am holding inside me and replace it with courage, dignity, self-confidence and the ambition to reach my goal.

Before I can adjust myself to this strange environment and get involved in things, I need friends who will help me overcome this urge to go home so I can accomplish my goal here in this unknown world which I entered.

Source: Virgil J. Vogel, *This Country Was Ours*

Indian Affairs set up a program called the Voluntary Relocation Program or Employment Assistance Program. Other programs offered by the Bureau of Indian Affairs paid for higher **education** (see p. 107) or training for those who relocated. During the decade, about 35,000 Native Americans moved to cities.

repatriation of remains

Return of Native American remains to tribal burial grounds. For over two centuries, Native American gravesites were disturbed for purposes of building or scientific research. Many bones ended up in museums across the country. The Smithsonian Institution alone held some 18,500 Native American remains. Until the 1970s, Native American protests against the treatment of their ancestors' graves were ignored. Finally, lawsuits were brought to return Native American remains to their homelands. Many *anthropologists* objected. They argued that the needs of science were more important than religious beliefs.

The **Native American Rights Fund (NARF)** (see p. 113) and American Indians Against Desecration have successfully repatriated

A Dinosaur Named Sue

The case of the dinosaur named Sue never reached the Supreme Court, but it was one of the strangest Native American legal cases of recent years. Sue is the largest, most complete *Tyrannosaurus rex* (*tuh-rahn-uh-SORE-us reks*) skeleton ever found. She was dug up in South Dakota in 1990 by fossil hunter Sue Hendrickson, from whom the skeleton got her name. The problem: the land from which the fossil was dug was on the Cheyenne River Sioux Reservation. Further, the land was the private property of a Sioux rancher, Maurice Williams, but was held in trust by the U.S. government. After 67 million years in the earth, the skeleton became the center of an ownership dispute among Hendrickson's fossil-hunting company, the Sioux, Williams, and the federal government. In the court's decision, an appeals court judge ruled that Sue was held in trust by the U.S. government for Williams. In 1997, Williams auctioned Sue to Chicago's Field Museum for $8.4 million—the most money ever paid for a fossil.

many sacred objects and remains. The American Committee for Preservation of Archeological Remains (ACPAR) opposes them. However, in 1990 the Native American Graves Protection and Repatriation Act was passed. This law required federal agencies and museums to return sacred objects and human remains to their original nations. In 1992, the last public display of ancient Native American remains closed. The display was at the Dickson Mounds Museum in Illinois. Native Americans have had some success in repatriating their ancestors' remains. However, they still face opposition from the scientific community.

self-determination policy

Plan that gives Native Americans the right to decide their own affairs. Native Americans and the federal government do not agree on the meaning of the term "self-determination." One way to define it is as the right of Native Americans to choose for themselves how to organize their societies and decide their futures, within a framework of federal assistance. This covers a wide area. It includes restoring the status of Native American nations and their governments, developing natural resources on reservations and other land, and beginning programs to improve the lives of Native Americans.

Support for self-determination began when some opposed the **termination policy** (see p. 119) of the 1950s and 1960s. Native American nations were not ready or able to switch from being dependent on the government to being independent. Without government support, some "terminated" nations fell into severe poverty. Termination policies also threatened Native American culture. As a result, many called for a reversal of government policy. It was proposed that Native American nations could exist with federal support. However, they could still determine their own internal political, economic, and social organization.

In 1970, President Richard Nixon formally cancelled the termination policy. Programs were set up to help Native Americans. Businesses, schools, and medical facilities were established. Since then, Native American nations have set up governments that operate independently yet within federal guidelines.

sports

Native Americans in the post-World War II era took part in competitive sports. Notable athletes include Northern Cheyenne judo champion and Olympic team member **Ben Nighthorse Campbell** (see p. 102). Campbell later became a U.S. senator. Another is Oglala Sioux distance runner Billy Mills. Mills won a surprise victory and set a world record in the 10,000-meter run in the 1964 Olympics. In group sports, the Iroquois National Lacrosse Team took part in the World Lacrosse Championships in 1990.

Several Native American groups have asked legislators and professional team owners to stop using Native American names for their teams or mascots. Offending team names include the Braves, Indians, and Redskins. As of the early 21st century, some local districts have passed laws that change school team names.

termination policy

Plan to end federal responsibility for Native American nations. Many government officials opposed restoring the status of Native American nations. There was also opposition from businesses. They wanted to profit from natural resources by building dams or mining minerals on Native American lands. Bills were introduced to abolish the reservation system. Many believed Native Americans should give up their **traditional ways** (see p. 120) and be assimilated into mainstream white society. One result of this attitude was to relocate native peoples to cities. Another was the proposal to terminate the *trust* relationship that existed between the federal government and Native American Nations. With this termination, Native Americans would no longer be dependent on the government. In 1949, the Hoover Commission on the Reorganization of Government rec-

The Terminator

On August 1, 1953, Congress passed House Concurrent Resolution 108, also known as the Termination Resolution. It declared that Congress intended to end "as rapidly as possible" the federal government's trust responsibility for Native Americans. As a start, it named certain states and certain nations to which this policy would apply.

[I]t is the policy of the Congress, as rapidly as possible, to make the Indians within the territorial limits of the United States subject to the same laws and entitled to the same privileges and responsibilities as are applicable to other citizens . . . to end their status as wards of the United States, and to grant them all the rights and prerogatives pertaining to American citizenship . . .

Source: Library of Congress

ommended termination. It also proposed the repeal of the **Indian Reorganization Act (IRA)** of 1934 (see p. 76), and the outlawing of 100 Native American nation constitutions.

In 1952, the federal government established a program to help Native Americans move to the cities. The following year the Termination Resolution was passed. It established a general policy of ending ***trust*** status for Native Americans. It said that it should begin "at the earliest possible time" in four states and with certain nations. The states named were California, Florida, New York, and Texas. The nations named were the Flathead of Montana, the Klamath of Oregon, the Menominee of Wisconsin, the Potawatomi (*pot-uh-WOT-uh-mee*) of Kansas and Nebraska, and the Chippewa on the Turtle Mountain Reservation, North Dakota.

Another law, passed in 1953, took another step toward ending the special trust status of reservations. It gave California, Minnesota, Nebraska, Oregon, and Wisconsin criminal and civil control over Native American lands, without the nations' consent.

With termination came the end of both treaty agreements and U.S. government responsibilities for the named nations and reservations. Between 1954 and 1962, 61 Native American nations were "terminated." The Menominee of Wisconsin fell into extreme poverty. They were unable to keep up a timber business and were forced to sell off land. They fought to get back their trust status and reservation status for the land they had left. This was granted by the Menominee Restoration Act of 1974. Four years later federal trust status was also restored to the Ottawa, Huron, Peoria, and Modoc.

There were others opposing the termination policy. Following the 1969 Josephy Report, a federal policy for Indian **self-determination** (see p. 118) was proposed. In 1977 the **American Indian Policy Review Commission** (see p. 100) recommended Indian self-determination. The Termination Resolution of 1953 was formally repealed, or canceled, in 1988.

traditional ways

Native cultural and spiritual practices. Since World War II, there has been increased interest in preserving traditional Native American culture. Native American nations have looked to **powwows** (see p. 115) as a time and place to honor the past and present and to find

A young boy from the Kwakiutl Nation in the Northwest proudly shows a traditional raven mask. (Courtesy of O. D. Neel)

meaning in their heritages. Also important have been efforts to teach native languages.

In their art, Native Americans have returned to using traditional materials and forms in their painting and sculpture. They have renewed their study and honor of the land. Many Native

Native American activists in Washington, D.C., during the Trail of Broken Treaties protest. (Denver Public Library)

Americans practice the rituals and beliefs of the Native American Church. Spiritual practices that have been revived during this period include the Sun Dance and the **Ghost Dance religion** (see p. 34). Native American culture has also been preserved through museums, such as the National Museum of the American Indian.

Trail of Broken Treaties

Political demonstration. In 1972, the **American Indian Movement (AIM)** (see p. 99) organized a demonstration. Its goal was to bring attention to the U.S. government's record on broken treaties with Native American nations. The plan was to take a caravan of cars, buses, and vans from San Francisco to Washington, D.C. Along the way, the caravan was joined by vehicles from many reservations. A paper concerning Native American rights was created. It was known as the Twenty Points. It was to be presented to government leaders. However, a meeting with Nixon administration official Harrison Loesch did not go well. The protestors took over the Bureau of Indian Affairs building. When the occupation ended, the government agreed to consider the Twenty Points. AIM leaders were later ***indicted*** for arson and grand larceny. They did, however, succeed in bringing Native American rights onto the national agenda.

tribal sovereignty *(SAHV-ren-tee)*
Concept defining Native American nations as individual nations entitled to a degree of self-rule. In the 19th century, Native Americans were forcibly removed to reservations. Next, efforts were

10 Largest Native American Nations

According to a 1995 report from the U.S. Bureau of the Census, the Cherokee are the largest American Indian tribe in the United States. With more than 300,000 members, they accounted for 19 percent of the Native American population in the 1990 census. Below are the top 10 tribes, from largest to smallest.

Rank	Nation	Number	Percent
1.	Cherokee	369.035	19.0
2.	Navajo	225,298	11.5
3.	Sioux	107,321	5.5
4.	Ojibwa	105.988	5.5
5.	Choctaw	86,231	4.5
6.	Pueblo	55,330	2.9
7.	Apache	53,330	2.8
8.	Iroquois	52,557	2.7
9.	Lumbee	50,888	2.6
10.	Creek	45,872	2.4

Source: U.S. Bureau of Census

made to end Native American communities and assimilate, or blend, Native Americans into American society. After 1934, this policy was reversed and Native American governments were recognized.

In the 1960s and 1970s, there was further acceptance of tribal sovereignty. There are now over 550 federally recognized nations with the right to regulate Native American membership, levy taxes, make laws, and control their own police and courts. The degree of self-government varies. In some instances, Native Americans are subject to four different forms of legal authority: federal law, state law, county or city law, and tribal law.

women's rights

Native American women made progress since World War II in achieving equality with men. They have gained greater influence in their communities. More women than ever received college educations. This led them to look for changes in the political system. Women were also aided by the passage of laws, such as the Economic Opportunity Act of 1964.

Activist Janet McCloud and others formed Women of All Red Nations (WARN) at the end of the 1970s. Their concerns have been with issues of domestic violence. They have also worked to renew the practice of native crafts.

Many non-Native American doctors worked for the Indian Health Service. They practiced involuntary sterilization of Native American women. Thousands of Native American women were sterilized without their knowledge. Leading the movement to end the practice was Cherokee physician Connie Uri (*YER-ee*).

By the 1990s, women gained leadership positions in business and among their nations. For example, Oklahoman Clara Sue Kidwell worked at the National Museum of the American Indian. Later, she began a Native American Studies program at the University of Oklahoma. Cherokee activist and author **Wilma Mankiller** (see p. 112) was the Principal Chief of the Cherokee Nation for a decade (1985-1995).

Wounded Knee, siege of

Confrontation between Native American activists and the U.S. government. In 1972 the **American Indian Movement (AIM)** (see p. 99) took over the Bureau of Indian Affairs (BIA) building in Washington, D.C. They occupied it for six days. After this incident, AIM leaders Russell Means and Dennis Banks returned to the Pine Ridge Reservation in South Dakota. Richard Wilson was the chairman of the Pine Ridge Native American council. He banned AIM activities and asked for U.S. marshals to protect BIA buildings. He also trained a police force using federal funds. These actions led the Sioux Civil Rights Organization to call for Wilson's impeachment. In 1973, more than 200 AIM members met at the site of the 1890 Wounded Knee massacre. They charged Wilson with corruption. They also accused the Native American government of working with the federal police. The FBI, U.S. Marshal Service, and BIA police soon surrounded them. More than 2,000 Native Americans came to Wounded Knee to support AIM. The 82nd Airborne Division prepared for possible military action.

This poster was created as a way of remembering the people who died at the original Wounded Knee massacre. (Private collection)

The siege of Wounded Knee lasted 71 days (February 27-May 8). During this time, two Native Americans were killed and a federal marshal was wounded. An end to the standoff was finally negotiated. Criminal charges were brought against 185 Native Americans, including Means and Banks. However, by 1974, most charges were dismissed.

Glossary

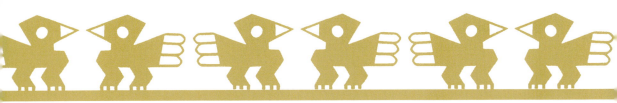

anthropologist: a scientist who studies human beings, especially their physical and cultural habits, customs, and relationships.

archeologist: a scientist who excavates, or carefully digs out, objects that have been buried in the ground. Archeologists try to learn about the cultures of people from the past by studying the remains of the ancient objects that belonged to them.

band: The form of political organization customarily found among hunter-gatherers. Bands usually have no permanent leaders; decisions are based on building consensus. Leadership tends to be situational, arising for short periods of time.

census: a survey done every four years by the U.S. government to count the nation's population. The census also measures various characteristics of the population, such as race, income, health, and education.

conflict of interest: a conflict between one's obligation to the public good and one's own benefit, as in the case of a government official who makes money by enforcing a certain government policy.

council house: a special building used for important decision-making meetings.

decathlon: an athletic contest in which competitors take part in 10 different events.

doctrine: a rule, principle, or theory of law.

epidemic: a contagious disease that becomes widespread throughout a community, making many people sick at the same time.

ethnologist: a special kind of anthropologist who specializes in comparing one culture to another.

geologist: a scientist who studies the physical nature and history of the earth, including forms of life found in fossils.

Indian agent: an official who represents the U.S. government in dealings with Native Americans.

indicted: charged with a crime.

integrated: a group that is not separated (or segregated) by racial or other differences.

irrigate: to water, by means of ditches or artificial channels or by sprinklers.

migration: the act of moving from one place to another, especially to leave one's homeland to settle in another.

militia: an army composed of regular citizens instead of professional soldiers.

nation: a stable community of people who have developed together from common ancestors over time and share territory, an economic way of life, a similar culture, and language. The word "nation" is sometimes considered to be interchangeable with the word "tribe." Some Native American peoples prefer one term to the other.

nomad: a member of a nation or tribe with no permanent home who moves from place to place hunting and gathering food.

pentathlon: an athletic contest in which competitors take part in five different events.

regulate: to control, direct, or govern according to a rule or law.

speculator: a person who buys land or other items of value hoping to take advantage of an expected rise or fall in the value of what they buy. Land speculators who purchased land inexpensively from Native Americans expected the land's value to increase quickly, if for example gold was found on the land or white settlers wished to move into the area.

title: when related to real estate, title refers to a right to land ownership.

trust: when referring to the legal term, a trust is property under the control of a trustee or administrator. In the case of Native American nations and the U.S. government, reservation land was set aside by the U.S. government for Native Americans, based on a "trust relationship" that the government would help maintain and improve the lives of those living on the reservations.

vaudeville: a stage show made up of a variety of acts, such as singing, dancing, comedy, acrobatics, and other forms of entertainment.

vocational: having to do with a trade or occupation. A vocational school is a school in which one learns the skills needed in specific trades.

war bonds: an interest-bearing certificate issued by the government to help raise funds to pay for the cost of a war.

ward: someone who is under the control of a guardian. For instance, in the "trust relationship" between Native Americans on the reservations and the United States, Native American peoples were seen as childlike "wards" of the government, rather than as equals.

Resources

General Subjects

Books

Aliki. *Corn Is Maize: The Gift of the Indians*. New York: Harper Collins, 1986.

Ancona, George. *Powwow*. San Diego, CA: Harcourt Brace Jovanovich, 1993.

Baquedano, Elizabeth. *Eyewitness: Aztec, Inca and Maya*. London and New York: DK Publishing, 2000.

Brown, Fern G. *American Indian Science: A New Look at Old Cultures*. New York: Twenty-First Century Books/Henry Holt and Co., 1997.

Caduto, Michael J., and Joseph Bruchac. *Keepers of the Earth: Native American Stories and Environmental Activities for Children*. Golden, CO: Fulcrum, 1988.

Erdoes, Richard. *The Rain Dance People: The Pueblo Indians, Their Past and Present*. New York: Alfred A. Knopf, 1976.

Fichter, George S. *American Indian Music and Musical Instruments*. New York: David McKay Co., 1978.

Gridley, Marion E. *American Indian Tribes*. New York: Dodd, Mead & Co., 1974.

Hirschfelder, Arlene B. *Happily May I Walk : American Indians and Alaska Natives Today.* New York: Scribner's, 1986.

Hofsinde, Robert (Gray-Wolf). *Indian Hunting*. New York: William Morrow and Company, 1962.

________. *Indian Sign Language*. New York: William Morrow and Co., 1960.

Hoyt-Goldsmith, Diane. *Pueblo Storyteller.* New York: Holiday House, 1991.

Jacobson, Daniel. *Indians of North America*. Danbury, CT: Franklin Watts, 1983.

Kavasch, E. Barrie, ed. *Native American Folklore, Activities and Foods*. Peterborough, NH: Cobblestone Publishing Inc., 1994.

La Pierre, Yvette. *Native American Rock Art: Messages from the Past.* Charlottesville, VA: Thomasson-Grant, Inc., 1994.

Liptak, Karen. *North American Indian Medicine People.* Danbury, CT: Franklin Watts, 1990.

________. *North American Indian Sign Language.* Danbury, CT: Franklin Watts, 1992.

________. *North American Indian Survival Skills.* Danbury, CT: Franklin Watts, 1990.

________. *North American Indian Tribal Chiefs.* Danbury, CT: Franklin Watts, 1992.

Mather, Christine. *Native America: Arts, Traditions, and Celebrations.* New York: Clarkson Potter Publishers, 1990.

McLuhan, T. C. *Touch the Earth: A Self-Portrait of Indian Existence.* New York: Simon and Schuster, 1971.

Murdoch, David. *Eyewitness Books: North American Indian.* New York: Alfred A. Knopf in association with the American Museum of Natural History, 1995.

Niethammer, Carolyn. *American Indian Food and Lore.* New York: Collier Books, 1974.

Ortiz, Simon. *The People Shall Continue.* San Francisco: Children's Book Press, 1988.

Prentaz, Scott. *Native American Culture: Tribal Law.* Vero Beach, FL: Rourke Publications, Inc., 1994.

Roberts, Chris. *Powwow Country.* Helena, MT: American and World Geographic Publishing, 1992.

Sherrow, Victoria. *Native American Culture: Spiritual Life.* Vero Beach, FL: Rourke Publications, Inc., 1994.

Tannenbaum, Beulah. *Science of the Early American Indians.* Danbury, CT: Franklin Watts, 1988.

Whitney, Alex. *Sports and Games the Indians Gave Us.* New York: David McKay Co., Inc., 1977.

Wolfson, Evelyn. *From Abenaki to Zuni: A Dictionary of Native American Tribes.* Illus. by William Sauls Bock (Delaware). New York: Walker Publishing Co., Inc., 1988.

________. *From the Earth to Beyond the Sky: Native American Medicine.* New York: Houghton Mifflin, 1993.

________. *Growing Up Indian.* New York: Walker and Company, 1986.

Wood, Marian. *Ancient America: Cultural Atlas for Young People.* New York: Facts on File, 1990.

________. *Myths and Civilization of the Native Americans.* New York: Peter Bedrick Books, 1998.

AUDIOCASETTES

The American Indian Oral History Collection. Ann Arbor, MI: Norman Ross Publishing Inc., 1977.

CD-ROM

Science through Native American Eyes. Kapaa, HI: Cradleboard Teaching Project, 1996.

VIDEO

Images of Indians (video series). Lethbridge, Alberta, Canada: Four Worlds Development Project, 1992.

Indians of North America (video series). Wynnewood, PA: Schlessinger Video Production, 1993–1994.

WEBSITES

American Indians: Apache, Blackfoot, Cherokee, Cheyenne, Lakota, and Pueblo: http://www.thewildwest.org/native_american/index.html

Edward S. Curtis's The North American Indian: Photographic Images: http://lcweb2.loc.gov/ammem/award98/ienhtml/tribes.html

Exploring Native Americans across the Curriculum: http://www.education-world.com/a_lesson/lesson038.shtml

The First Americans: http://www.germantown.k12.il.us/html/intro.html

The First Americans: Dineh, Muskogee, Tlingit, Lakota, Iroquois: http://www.u.arizona.edu/ic/kmartin/School/index.htm

First Nations Compact History: http://www.dickshovel.com/up.html

National Museum of the American Indian: http://www.nmai.si.edu/

Native American Website for Children: http://www.nhusd.k12.ca.us/ALVE/NativeAmerhome.html/nativeopeningpage.html

Native North America:
http://www.anthro.mankato.msus.edu/cultural/northamerica/index.shtml

NativeWeb: http://www.nativeweb.org/

WWW Virtual Library - American Indians: http://www.hanksville.org/NAresources/

History and Biography

(Since 1839)

Books

Ashabranner, Brent. *To Live in Two Worlds: American Indian Youth Today*. New York: Dodd Mead, 1984.

Freedman, Russell. *Indian Chiefs*. New York: Holiday House, 1987.

Hall, Moss. *Go Indians! Stories of the Great Indian Athletes of the Carlisle School*. Ward Ritchie Press, 1971.

Jacobson, Daniel. *Young Jim Thorpe: All American Athlete*. Mahwah, NJ: Troll Associates, 1996.

Waldman, Carl. *Who Was Who in Native American History*. New York: Facts on File, 1990.

Wood, Ted, with Wanbli Numpa Afraid of Hawk. *A Boy Becomes a Man at Wounded Knee*. New York: Walker and Company, 1992.

Video

The West: Speck of the Future (Episode Three). Washington, DC: The West Film Project and WETA, 2001.

The West: Death Runs Riot (Episode Four). Washington, DC: The West Film Project and WETA, 2001.

The West: The Grandest Enterprise under God (Episode Five). Washington, DC: The West Film Project and WETA, 2001.

The West: Fight No More Forever (Episode Six). Washington, DC: The West Film Project and WETA, 2001.

The West: The Geography of Hope (Episode Seven). Washington, DC: The West Film Project and WETA, 2001.

The West: One Sky above Us (Episode Eight). Washington, DC: The West Film Project and WETA, 2001.

Websites

Carlisle Indian Industrial School: http://home.epix.net/~landis/

National Portrait Gallery: Native Americans—Billy Bowlegs: http://www.npg.si.edu/col/native/bowlegs.htm

National Portrait Gallery: Native Americans—Chief Joseph: http://www.npg.si.edu/col/native/joseph.htm

National Portrait Gallery: Native Americans—Geronimo: http://www.npg.si.edu/col/native/geronimo.htm

The Trial of Standing Bear: http://score.rims.k12.ca.us/activity/standingbear/

Folklore, Fiction, and Poetry

Books

Bierhorst, John. *The Woman Who Fell from the Sky: The Iroquois Story of Creation.* New York: Morrow, 1993.

Bruchac, Joseph. *Flying with the Eagle, Racing the Great Bear; Stories from Native North America.* BridgeWater Books, 1993.

Cannon, A. E. *The Shadow Brothers.* New York: Delacorte Press, 1990.

Cohlene, Terri. *Clamshell Boy: A Makah Legend.* Mahwah, NJ: Troll, 1991.

Dorris, Michael. *Morning Girl.* New York: Hyperion, 1992.

Esbensen, Barbara. *The Star Maiden: An Ojibway Tale.* Boston: Little, Brown, 1988.

Goble, Paul. *Brave Eagle's Account of the Fetterman Fight.* Lincoln: University of Nebraska Press (Bison Books), 1992.

________. *Iktomi and the Ducks*. New York: Orchard Books, 1990.

Green, Richard G. (Mohawk). *A Wundoa Book: "I'm Number One."* Sacramento, CA: Ricara Features, 1980.

Greene, Jacqueline Dembar. *Manabozho's Gifts: Three Chippewa Tales*. Boston: Houghton Mifflin, 1994.

Lavitt, Edward, and Robert E. McDowell. *Nihancan's Feast of Beaver: Animal Tales of the North American Indians*. Santa Fe, NM: Museum of New Mexico Press, 1990.

Mayo, Gretchen Will. *Earthmaker's Tales: North American Indian Stories about Earth Happenings*. New York: Walker Publishing Company, 1989.

________. *Star Tales: North American Indian Stories about the Stars*. New York: Walker Publishing Company, 1987.

Medicine Story (Manitonquat). *The Children of the Morning Light: Wampanoag Tales*. New York: Macmillan, 1994.

Osofsky, Audrey. *Dreamcatcher*. New York: Orchard Books, 1992.

Robinson, Margaret A. *A Woman of Her Tribe*. New York: Scribner's, 1990.

San Souci, Robert. *Sootface: An Ojibwa Cinderella Story*. Illus. by Daniel San Souci. New York: Delacorte, 1994.

Sneve, Virginia Driving Hawk, ed. *Dancing Teepees: Poems of American Indian Youth*. New York: Holiday House, 1989.

Two Bulls, Marty Grant. *Ptebloka: Tails from the Buffalo*. Vermillion, SD: Dakota Books, 1991.

Viola, Herman, general ed. *American Indian Stories*. Milwaukee: Raintree Publishers, 1990.

Selected Bibliography

Billard, Jules B., ed. *The World of the American Indian.* Washington, DC: National Geographic Society, 1974.

Brown, Dee. *Bury My Heart at Wounded Knee: An Indian History of the American West.* New York: Henry Holt & Co., 2001.

Capps, Benjamin. *The Great Chiefs.* Alexandria, VA: Time-Life Books, 1975.

Catlin, George. *Letters and Notes on the Manners, Customs, and Conditions of North American Indians.* New York: Dover Publications, 1985.

Collins, Richard, ed. *The Native Americans: The Indigenous People of North America.* New York: Smithmark Publishers, 1991.

Jhoda, Gloria. *Trail of Tears.* San Antonio, TX: Wings Press, 1995.

Josephy, Alvin, Jr. *500 Nations: An Illustrated History of North American Indians.* New York: Alfred A. Knopf, 1994.

Kopper, Philip. *The Smithsonian Book of North American Indians Before the Coming of the Europeans.* Washington, DC: Smithsonian Books, 1986.

Lavender, David. *The Great West.* Boston: Houghton Mifflin Company, 1987.

Matthiessen, Peter. *In the Spirit of Crazy Horse.* New York: Penguin USA, 1992.

Nabokov, Peter. *Native American Testimony: A Chronicle of Indian-White Relations from Prophecy to the Present, 1492–2000.* New York: Penguin USA, 1999.

Smith, Carter. *The Explorers and Settlers: A Sourcebook on Colonial America.* Brookfield, CT: Millbrook Press, 1991.

Tanner, Helen Hornbeck. *The Settling of North America: The Atlas of the Great Migrations into North America from the Ice Age to the Present.* New York: Macmillan, 1995.

Taylor, Colin F. *Native American Arts and Crafts.* London: Salamander Books, 1995.

Waldman, Carl. *Who Was Who in Native American History.* New York: Facts on File, 1990.

Ward, Geoffrey. *The West: An Illustrated History.* Boston: Little Brown and Company, 1996.

Index

Note: The index below contains entries for both volumes of the Student Almanac of Native American History. *The boldfaced number 1 refers to pages in the first volume. The boldfaced number 2 refers to pages in the second volume.*

L

M

N

O

P

T

U

W

Y